The Positive Charge

Six Positive Connections to Success

Beverly Sallee

SUCCESS **DNA**

A SuccessDNA Publication

A SuccessDNA Nonfiction Book

Page design: Megan Hughes, Eh? Clerical Services Inc.
Cover design: www.meshcreative.com

SuccessDNA, Inc.
COPYRIGHT 2004, Beverly Sallee
All Rights Reserved
Printed in the United States of America
10 9 8 7 6 5 4 3 2 1

Library of Congress Control No: Applied For
ISBN No. 0-9746844-5-7

SUCCESS DNA is a trademark of Success DNA, Inc.

To my parents

Who taught me early

To be an entrepreneur

And believed in my abilities to succeed.

In keeping with the foundational principles I learned from my parents about helping others I would like to donate a portion of the proceeds of this book to the Ambassador Fund to help children in crisis.

The Positive Charge

Preface
Connecting Yourself to Success

I don't know what success is for your life. But I do know this:

I know that deep down inside, you have an intuitive understanding of what is success. I discovered for myself what success means in my life and in the lives of thousands if not tens of thousands of people I've met in the last twenty years.

Success for me and for them has been starting a business of our own—one that we developed at our own initiative and one from which we have received great rewards.

Success for me has been a business that puts me in daily contact with highly positive, motivated people who share my value system. Success for me has been involvement in a business that has a highly positive financial profile—a business that offers quality products and services at very competitive prices and good profit margin—as well as an opportunity to make a significant positive difference in a need-filled world. Success for me has been a business that keeps me thinking positive, speaking positive, acting positive—and in all ways, cultivating positive relationships with people I meet on a daily basis. Success on these levels is electric for me, a positive charge.

I like the way I live...the money I earn...and most of all, who I am as a person. That's positive! And for me, it's the very best life.

This book is about discovering and pursuing "The Positive Charge" in your life. I encourage you now to adopt this mind set: Choose carefully what you do with your time and energy. Choose to be positively charged. Choose to connect yourself to success. And once you have determined what is positively best for you...get going in hot pursuit of it!

— Beverly Sallee

PART I

Positive Direction

Chapter 1
Everybody Has a Dream Hidden in Their Heart

What does the word "dream" mean to you?

I asked a group of people this question and here are some of the responses I received:

- ❖ Freedom
- ❖ Travel
- ❖ Hope
- ❖ Time
- ❖ Choices
- ❖ Security
- ❖ Fishing—on a Tuesday when nobody else is at the fishing hole
- ❖ Free of credit card debt
- ❖ Sleep
- ❖ Having Mondays off
- ❖ A new car
- ❖ A new house
- ❖ Plenty of money to pay cash for college tuition

The fact is, everybody has a dream hidden in their heart.

A dream is beyond a need. Our needs may drive us to one level of success, but it's our dreams that drive us higher and higher.

My First Dream is Not My Current Dream

My first dream in life was to be a concert pianist. I worked very hard on that goal while I was in college. Not only did I take a full load of classes, but also I worked thirty hours a week and practiced piano four hours a day. I was determined to get a degree and forge a career in music. I graduated magna cum laude with a music degree in piano and felt as if I was on my way.

Things didn't turn out exactly as I had planned. I married, took a couple of detours in life, finished a master's degree in choral conducting, and by the time someone first approached me about developing a business of my own, I had two young children—ages four and seven—and was teaching full-time in a college.

I was very discouraged and disillusioned. I had done everything I knew to do to prepare myself for a career, was teaching full-time plus teaching some night classes as a part-time second job, and had thirty-five private piano students. I directed community theater on Saturday and on Sunday, I played the organ and conducted the church choir. I was busy.

And...I was broke. I traded piano lessons for wood to heat our home and for other services that I needed for my two children—such as haircuts and babysitting and fabric from which I could sew clothes.

In the summers, I went out to the nearby orchards to pick fruit. The farmers would sell boxes of fruit for very little money if the customer would pick the fruit himself. I'd take that fruit home and can it for eating the following winter. My record is 134 quarts of peaches canned in one day. On rainy days, I went to pick strawberries because on rainy days, the farmers would sell us strawberries for five cents a pound. One day I picked seventy-five pounds of strawberries—and let me assure you, that's a lot of strawberries. They only cost me $3.75. I stayed up all night freezing them and making jam.

When I first was presented with the opportunity for a network marketing business, I frankly didn't believe all the big numbers that were used in the presentation. Earn fifty thousand dollars a year? Who were they kidding? I was working very hard and not coming any place close to earning that kind of money. But, when someone told me that I could earn $400 a month...that hit home.

My bills at the time were about $1200 a month and I was making $800 a month teaching full-time at the college. I didn't need a course in math to tell me that this business might be a way I could earn the additional money I needed without teaching nights and having thirty-five private piano students. I was willing to work hard—I simply needed to be shown how to trade out one kind of effort for another kind of effort that had a bigger pay-back potential.

I took the hours that I had been devoting to teaching on an hourly wage and used those hours to make presentations that had the potential for not only bringing me immediate cash, but of bringing me even more cash down the line. I worked part-time...started small...and stayed at it. I needed to.

No, I didn't have grandiose dreams at the beginning. I just wanted to make enough money to pay my bills so that I'd be even with the world at the end of every month.

What Do YOU Want?

What do you want? For the vast majority of people, "want" is related to something they believe to be desirable and good...but they don't have it right now. "Want" is just beyond their reach, just beyond this moment.

I don't know what you want...but I know this—you want something. Every person has desires and dreams. You may have buried your desires and dreams or tried to stuff them deep within, thinking your particular desire or dream can never come true. You may have been beaten down by so many adverse situations or circumstances that you hardly remember your desires and dreams.

Take time to reevaluate and rekindle what you truly want. If you are going to succeed in a business of your own, you need to know WHY you are in business. You need to know what you hope to get out of that business.

Ask Yourself Three Questions

I encourage you to ask yourself three very important questions as you consider the reason you are in business or are considering starting a business:

Question 1: What kind of lifestyle do I want to lead?

<u>Question 2: Is my current way of earning money going to get me to that lifestyle?</u>

A good way to answer this question is to look around at others who are earning money in the manner you are and take a look at the lifestyle they are leading.

<u>Question 3: What is required for me to get to the lifestyle I want to lead?</u>

If the answer to the second question above is "no," then take a look at people who are living a life comparable to the one you want to life and ask yourself, "What did they do to get to this position in their life and how long did it take?"

The fastest way I know to a quality lifestyle and high level of income is to be a business owner.

If YOUR Dream is Going to Come True...It Will Be the Result of What YOU Decide to Do.

Chapter 2
How Much Do You Really Love Your Current Job?

Several years ago I read an article in the New York Times that was headlined, "What Ever Happened to Easy Street?" The article reported that in 1986, the average person in our nation thought that if he made fifty thousand dollars a year, he'd be on "easy street." The conclusion drawn by the article was this: Somebody moved the street!

Most people need to face a grim reality that they are no closer to financial independence and an easier life today than they were last year...or five years ago...or a couple of decades ago.

The vast majority of the people I've met through the years grew up with the idea that if they stayed out of trouble and made good grades, they could and would go to college...and in college, if they studied hard and learned a "career," they'd get a good job when they got out of college...and once on the job, if they worked hard and worked smart, they'd advance to the point where life wasn't merely affordable, but life was sprinkled with a few luxuries. That's been the American dream for decades.

The sad reality is that it just isn't so for many, many people.

I followed this dream until I was in my mid-thirties.

I taught high school music for several years and thought: If I could just get a job in a college, I'd be better off. So I started a doctoral program, got a job in a college, and found that I was no better off.

I had a bachelor's degree in piano and a master's degree in choral conducting. I thought I had done everything possible to prepare myself for a career in music, and I felt certain that career would result in sufficient financial rewards for me to live a comfortable life. I was wrong. Teaching music, even at the college level, did not provide for me the financial compensation that I needed to raise two children, and to do so in a manner that was not only enriching to my children, but comfortable and rewarding to me. I was barely scraping by—our life was hardly what I wanted for myself and my children, much less what I might have dreamed about.

I loved teaching.

I loved music.

I loved my students and seeing them excel in their performances.

But I did not love the financial rewards that I received from teaching music, and therefore, I did not truly love my job. A big part of loving the work you do is enjoying the rewards of the work you do.

How Much Would it Take for You to Leave Your Job?

An important question for you to answer is this: If you knew your bills were paid and your income was on the rise from a source other than your present job, how excited would you feel about getting up and going to work every day?

I have met literally hundreds of people who have answered that question "not very excited" or "not excited at all."

There are several wonderful benefits of being an independent business owner and doing work that you do enjoy doing and that is financially rewarding. Let me give you five of them:

Reason 1: Job Security

A banker called me one day and told me that without any warning, she had been let go from her job. So had a number of other people at the bank. She was in shock. She had worked for this particular bank for twenty years and had never had a negative comment made to her by a supervisor or a customer. Her employer told her that she had been a model employee, but that the bank was streamlining some parts of its operation and that her job position was being eliminated. "Job position" and "job," of course, were one and the same to this banker!

The good news about being in business for yourself is that you can't be laid off. If you work and produce, you earn! You have job security according to your definition, not someone else's.

Reason 2: No Discrimination

We like to think we live in a world that doesn't discriminate against age, race, or gender. That just isn't so. The discrimination may be more subtle today than in past decades but it exists nonetheless.

"You can be replaced" is the mantra of many supervisors. The phrase is intended to motivate. I don't know about you, but that phrase has never motivated me. Rather, it sends a message to me of "you aren't valued," "you aren't important," "you aren't appreciated."

There is minimal discrimination in most direct-sales businesses. People are far more likely to evaluate you according to your performance than any other external standard.

Furthermore, if you produce, you can't be replaced! Actually, in network marketing, your goal in your business is to replace yourself with a hundred, two hundred, or more other people who do what you do under you, in various networking organizations, so that you benefit from what they do. The eventual goal of just about everybody I know is to completely replace themselves with consumers and salesmen and recruiters many times over. You, however, are the business owner and you decide when you have been replaced enough times!

Reason 3: No Ceiling on Income

If you work for someone other than yourself, your salary is dictated by someone else. You may think that you can advance and earn what you'd like to make financially, but it just isn't so. You will never make more than your company—and sometimes your boss or immediate supervisor—think you should make. And what they think you should make is always significantly less than what they make.

Your employer or supervisor in a traditional job controls a great deal of your life. Your boss very likely determines your salary...the amount of free time you have (or stated another way, the amount of time you need to spend on the job to be considered a worthy team player who is contributing a hundred percent)...and the amount of freedom you have to express your own creativity and ideas as part of your work. In determining your salary, your boss indirectly determines how many children you have, what kind of car you drive, what kind of college you will be able to send your children to, and what kind of house you live in (which includes what kind of neighborhood you live in and therefore, in many instances, the schools your children attend when they are young). Your boss determines when and for how long you can take a vacation with your family. Ultimately, your boss has a very strong say in when you can retire and at what income level.

There's no ceiling on what you can earn when you are in business for yourself.

Reason 4: Effort Results in Reward

One of the frequent complaints of employees in traditional corporate, retail, and manufacturing jobs is that they often work very hard without much reward, and those who are hard-working, are sometimes very frustrated when they look at their peers and see people who are earning what they are earning for far less effort or quality performance.

I've always worked hard. And I don't mind telling you that I resented at times the fact that I seemed to be working twice as hard as some of the people around me who were earning the same salary I was receiving. Until recently, the idea of merit pay wasn't associated with teaching. Believe me, I've met some very hard-working teachers in my time...and I've also met a few who were lazy. It's tough to stay excited about your job if you see an inequity in the amount of effort being put out and the amount of pay coming in.

In direct sales, hard work generates business and business generates income. The more calls you make, the more presentations you make, the more sales you make, and the more income you make. Those who work hard are rewarded well. There's no inequity based upon any other factor than performance. It doesn't matter who's in with the boss, who's related to the supervisor's cousin, what a person looks like, or what a person's ethnic, cultural, or racial background may be.

Reason 5: Ongoing Productivity

Most owners of small businesses feel that they have to be at the shop for productivity, quality, sales, and morale to remain high. I have met a number of small-business owners who rarely if ever take vacations because they fear their business will fall apart in their absence.

Let me briefly point out the difference between self-employment and owning a business of your own. I like what Robert Kiyosaki said in his best-selling book *Cash Flow Quadrant* on this issue. He pointed out that a business owner who creates a network marketing business can build residual income over time based primarily on reordered products or renewed services, and the salesmanship of others. A self-employed person's business is dependent entirely on their individual personal performance—usually one job after the next after the next.

In a marketing network, your business is designed and engineered to succeed without your immediate presence or personal input. Each network you establish should go on without your constant attention to every detail. Most direct-sales corporations have mentoring programs to help you achieve just that level of smooth-flowing operation.

Quick to Quit!

When I knew that my bills were paid and I had extra money at the end of the month just from my part-time direct-sales business income...I wasn't nearly as excited about getting up to give music-history lectures at seven-thirty in the morning three times a week. I wasn't nearly as interested in listening to my "boss" make demands on my upcoming weekends. I certainly wasn't very interested in what my boss had to say to me at "raise-consideration" interviews.

I became far more independent!

That didn't mean I enjoyed music...teaching...or young people any less. I still love all three and am still very active in music, teaching, and youth programs—just not as a full-time job.

I found another job I truly love!

Do What You Love and Love All Aspects of What You Do.

Chapter 3
Are You Willing to Try Something New?

Almost everybody I know has a "my ancestor could have had it made" story. One woman told me, "My great uncle sold his acreage of orange trees in Anaheim just three years before Walt Disney announced plans to build a place called Disneyland. His property was only two miles away. He could have been rich." Another person told me, "My great-grandfather had an opportunity to buy that property for only $100 an acre." He was pointing to land that is now filled with downtown skyscrapers in one of the largest cities in the Northwest.

There are opportunities available to you today that just may go down in your family folklore—stories that could be told from the angle, "My ancestor could have made it big," or stories that could be told, "My ancestor saw a fabulous opportunity and jumped on it." Which will it be?

It is kind of like learning to surf.

One of my dreams a number of years ago was to learn how to surf. I acted on that dream. I rented out my house for the summer, sold my car, bought a ticket to Hawaii, rented a cheap apartment in Waikiki, rented a cheap car, bought a surfboard, and learned to surf.

I decided I was going to learn how to surf or die trying. I went out the first morning with my ten-foot Phil Edwards board, paddled out beyond the reef, and began to paddle away to try to catch the next wave.

I learned very quickly that you don't catch every wave. It takes good upper-body strength to paddle long and fast to catch a wave. My first hours out in the surf were spent doing a lot of paddling and a lot of missing the waves that came surging out of the vast expanse of ocean behind me. But oh, the joy that came the first time I felt that rush of water behind me pushing me toward the shoreline! I had caught a wave! Never mind trying to stand up. I just tried to hang on, flat on my stomach, and I managed to hang onto that board all the way to the shore.

Several times later, I caught a wave and I was able to get up on my knees. Progress!

Soon—but not immediately—I had ridden enough times on my knees to have the courage to try standing up.

Did I fall? You bet.

Did I get back up and try again? Absolutely.

There was a process involved in learning to surf, and there's a process involved in learning how to do anything that really matters in this life. One doesn't become a surfer by looking cute in a bathing suit, renting a surfboard, and automatically riding the first wave to the shore. One doesn't become a successful business person by buying a briefcase and signing a million-dollar deal on his or her first sales call.

Part of the process involves practicing the basic "moves" of whatever it is that you are pursuing. If you are pursuing a career in sales, you need to be making calls—there's no substitute for getting referrals and making calls...and getting referrals and making calls...and getting referrals and making calls. No matter how successful you become, your business will continue to grow and develop because you are doing the basics of getting referrals and making calls.

Part of the process involves practice. I learned the first day out in the surf that surfing was going to take a lot of practice. But as the days went by, I also learned that the more I paddled, the stronger my upper body muscles became. The stronger I became, the better able I was to catch the waves. The sooner I caught a wave, the better positioned I was for maintaining my balance. And, the better my balance, the longer the ride. Ultimately, the more I practiced, the better I got.

The same will be true for you. The more you practice your sales pitch...the more you make presentations...the more you listen to motivating tapes and attend motivating seminars...the more you will be strengthened as a person, the easier you'll find it to talk about your business and close a sale, the better equipped you will be to face challenges as you go along, and ultimately, the greater the success you will experience.

From time to time, the process may involve dealing with a competitor who doesn't play fair. I was headed for the shore one day when I noticed a young man heading straight for me on his surfboard. He was going to cut me off! I later realized that his action was not a matter of carelessness or a failure to see me. He had intentionally sought to cut me off to show me that he was the king of that stretch of the beach. Well...he didn't know how much I did NOT want to be knocked off my surfboard! As he got close to me and I realized we were about to collide, I reached out my hand and literally shoved him away from me so we wouldn't collide. He went tumbling off his board. As he paddled back out to the sea, he called to his surfing buddies, "Don't mess with the big haole on the white board!"

There may be times when you need to send a strong signal to those who are trying to horn into your territory, take over your department, invade your turf, or steal your rightfully gained position that you will not be intimidated and you will not be conquered. There are times to fight to maintain the quality or quantity of what you've built or to defend what you know is rightfully yours.

Warnings Before Take-Off

In the course of my travels, I've heard just about every announcement that an airline pilot can make. One pilot informed us over the intercom that he was behind a locked door and had an axe in the cockpit with him. Another told us that if any passenger did anything funny, he was going to turn the plane upside down and fly that way until things were put in order. I wasn't quite sure how the stewardesses and others were going to bring order to a planeload of people that was flying upside down, but I could tell he was serious in his warning.

Perhaps the best pilot warning that I heard, however, was the one in which a pilot told us that we were not to congregate in the aisles or toward the front of the plane. He went so far as to suggest that if anybody was standing in the aisle outside the pilot's door, the passengers in the first-class section should feel free to restrain that person. Well, the restroom was also located toward the front of that particular model of plane! Nobody stood up in first class that entire flight—it was a three-hour flight and nobody in first class dared to use the restroom!

There are several things I want to warn you about before you launch into a direct marketing or other business of your own.

Warning 1: There's a Big Difference Between a Dream and a Daydream

Dreams are the soil for goals and plans. They are something you can chart your way toward reaching. Daydreams, by comparison, are idle whims and wishes.

So many people live in a state of "If Only."

They sigh as they say…

"If only I had decided to become a doctor instead of a musician…"

"If only I had finished school…"

"If only I had invested in real estate a few years ago…"

"If only I had saved ten percent of my income two decades ago…"

"If only I had invested in computer stock back when computers were new…"

"If only I hadn't let those credit cards get out of hand…"

Living in an "If Only" state is not only unproductive, it's demoralizing! It's living in the past and second-guessing life. There's nothing forward-moving or motivating about the "If Only" state.

I used to dream about ways of making more money. Some of my ideas also were in the realm of "If Only."

"If only I could invent something that everybody wanted…"

"If only I could produce something that everybody wants at a much cheaper price…"

"If only I could find a rich co-investor..."

I'd daydream about where I'd be in my life if I had invented the ballpoint pen or the paper clip or the stapler! Alas...I hadn't invented anything and my daydreams took me nowhere.

If you truly are going to succeed in a business of your own, you need to make sure your dream is something that you can plot your way toward achieving. It needs to be rooted in the reality of hard work, smart decisions, and a great deal of flexibility and learning.

<u>Warning 2: You'll Have to Give Up Your Excuses</u>

Early one morning I was sitting in the Philadelphia airport in anticipation of a flight. Looking out the window, I watched a beautiful shiny 747 airplane being pulled into position by a very small little tractor!

As long as that plane was tied to the tractor, it was in no position to fly. Even though it was far larger and more powerful than the tractor, the plane could release none of its potential while it was being towed by that tractor.

That's the way many people are when it comes to the excuses they have for why they aren't more productive. They are led around by their excuses.

"The yard needed to be mowed."

"The dog needed to be taken to the park."

"I don't have time for this."

"My house needed to be vacuumed."

"My spouse didn't want me to go..."

"We just aren't business people."

"It won't work here."

"We're not quite ready for that kind of business in this part of the country."

"People just don't know enough to be able to do this—nobody will understand this."

The excuses are always the same in every expanding market I've ever encountered, both in the United States and overseas. These were the excuses that were voiced when the personal computer first hit the marketplace in the early 1980s.

It doesn't matter if you are high-tech, low-tech, or no-tech...people still want stuff in their lives—they especially want products that will help them get around faster, do things easier, finish tasks quicker, get information with less effort, enjoy life more fully, and get more for their money. They want to benefit from technology and use technology, even if they don't have a clue how a particular technology works, much less how to repair it when it breaks.

I know a woman who has a business in Idaho. She drove all the way to the coast of Oregon—difficult driving for nearly ten hours in the snow—to meet with me. She told me how she had mounted a satellite dish on a small house trailer, and was traveling across eastern Oregon and western Idaho selling satellite dishes to every person she encountered. She didn't make calls in advance. She just drove into people's ranches and into their driveways as if to say, "I'm here! Look what I have! Don't you want one, too?" She didn't feel the least bit disadvantaged because she lived in a sparsely populated area or that she sometimes had to drive twenty miles before she found her next potential customer. She saw the rural and remote environment as giving her an advantage in selling the particular product she was offering.

And, while she was there making sure these folks had the opportunity to be connected to the world with a satellite dish, she sold them other products that were offered by her organization! Most of these people were thrilled to think they could have the products delivered directly to them without their having to drive into town to shop.

That means, of course, that this woman sometimes needs to drive as much as eight hours to pick up product and then deliver it. Nevertheless, she does so and her business is growing. People who see the level of service she gives often are willing to buy much more product, or to tell their friends who aren't on her path about her products and personal-delivery service.

Many people I know would think it absolutely impossible to build a business in the remote area where this woman works. But she's doing it! And with computers and Internet capabilities, building a business in a remote area has become all that much easier for just about every person.

It's the excuses—not the circumstances—that will always keep you from releasing your full potential in your business. They will run your life, rather than your dreams and goals running your life.

One or the other will be in charge—your goals, or your excuses. One or the other will dictate how you spend your time, energy, and resources.

<u>Warning 3: You're Going to Need to Make Some Changes in Your Use of Time</u>

Every person has time. For example, a network-marketing business is never a matter of "if a person has time." The truth is, we all have time. We all have twenty-four hours in a day and eight thousand, seven hundred, and sixty hours in a year. We all have ten thousand and eighty minutes in a week. No...it's not about time. It's about what we believe we should do with our time.

Any business start-up is always a decision rooted in what you believe about yourself and what you believe you can achieve and should achieve in this life. It's about what you want to accomplish and how you want live.

Are you excited enough about the potential you see that you are willing to rearrange your schedule and adjust your priorities?

Are you enthusiastic enough about the realization of your own dreams and potential?

Are you willing to set aside some hours, or trade out some hours if you see good success from your effort?

No one controls your time but you. You have chosen the commitments you have made of your time. Are you willing to make some new choices?

Think of your time as a means of investment. Every person is an investor whether he or she knows it or not. You are investing your time in something. You are investing your energy and talent and creativity in something. You are also investing your money in something.

The key question you need to ask is this: Am I investing my time, energy, talents, skills, and money in something that will give me the return I desire on my investment?

If you invest your time talking on the phone to your girlfriends, rehashing all the old gossip again and again, you aren't going to have much to show for your time at the end of the day—and ultimately, you probably have done nothing of substance truly to enrich your friendships. If you invest your money going to a movie or out to a club, you may have an enjoyable and relaxing time—and we do need those times in our life—but you will have done nothing to influence the world, earn a return on your investment, or contribute to your own self-betterment.

Warning 4: You Are Going to Have to Readjust Your Focus

You are going to have to make a decision that you are going to pursue your potential. Many people spend their days doing chores and working at tasks that other people are requiring them to do to fulfill their potential.

My challenge to you is this: At what point are you going to stop trying to please everybody else and start pleasing yourself?

I'm not talking about being self-centered or self-absorbed.

I'm not talking about being prideful or motivated only by "looking out for number one."

Rather, I'm talking about your pursuing what you truly believe are your God-given dreams, ambitions, and goals—those things that are a part of your ultimate reason for being on this earth.

Taking Off Requires ACTING on a Decision

A pilot can sit in the cockpit of an airplane and think about taking off for hours. The pilot may adjust all the dials, talk to the control tower personnel, and prepare the passengers. But until that pilot pulls back the levers and begins to roll the plane down the runway, there's no flight.

Don't put off making a decision about your future. Check out various opportunities and spend enough time doing your homework. Make certain that you truly can be excited about the product you are selling. Then, make a decision! Don't "toy" with the idea. If you can't quit thinking about the possibilities or the product line...jump in!

Don't Wait for Your Ship to Come In. Swim Out to Meet It.

PART II

Positive Preparation

Chapter 4

Well, Yes, You ARE in Business to Make Money

Why Are You Starting This Business?

If you answer that question with any answer other than "to make money," then you aren't truly interested in starting a business. The purpose of a business is to make money!

What you do with that money is something else. The reason you want money will give you the motivation to start your business and give you staying power in the face of rejection, slow times, and times when you feel weary and stressed out.

Through the years, I've discovered in my work with literally thousands of business associates that the stronger and clearer the reason a person wants more money directly determines the success a person achieves and the rate he or she achieves it. Note those two words: stronger and clearer. Your reason for wanting more money must be very deeply held in your heart. The more desperate a person is to change his or her circumstances...the greater the need...the stronger the desire to have what one doesn't have...the more compelling the goal...the deeper the emotions associated with a desire to make a difference...then the greater the motivation and the greater the success. The person who sincerely wants to succeed in any business is the person who will find a way to succeed. He or she will do what it takes.

The reason for needing more money must be one that is very clear to the person starting the business. It needs to be obvious to that person even if it isn't obvious to anyone else. There's no room for "might be," "could be," "sorta is," or "kinda," when it comes to your reason. There's no room for vague feelings and wishes. You should be able to state very clearly, "I'm starting this business to make money, and I want more money because _____" and then fill in that blank with fewer than ten words.

It Takes Money to Pay Bills and Erase Debt

One of the best reasons I know to make more money is to pay bills and get out of debt.

Many people I know started this New Year with a hangover—it wasn't necessarily a hangover from too much alcohol, but rather, a hangover of debt. They carried into the New Year bills still owed from the previous year.

One of the foremost goals I hope you have for developing a business of your own is this: Get out of debt.

I have met countless adults who have been in some form of debt all of their adult life. They graduated from college with school loans to repay. In some cases, even before they graduated, they had acquired credit cards and were in credit card debt. Before long they had taken out loans to buy a car or some other item they desired.

The sad fact is this: The vast majority of people never get completely out of debt—rather, their personal indebtedness is likely to increase. I recently read a study in which people who were in their early forties were asked to identify their income now, five years ago, ten years ago, and fifteen years ago. In nearly every case, income had increased fairly steadily over the last fifteen years. All of them were making considerably more now than fifteen years ago.

They then were asked to identify their level of personal debt—now, five years ago, ten years ago, and fifteen years ago. In nearly every case, their debt load had also increased fairly steadily over the last fifteen years. In fact, it had risen at a rate greater than their income.

Now its one thing to be paying in time installments on a house or a piece of land—I don't consider that debt, I consider that to be an investment. What you are purchasing is likely to increase your net worth, not decrease it. The debt about which I am concerned is the personal debt that is for items a person already has and is using, but for which the person has not yet paid. For example, a young man admitted to me recently that he's several thousand dollars in debt to a department store. I asked him what he had purchased at the store and he admitted very wryly, "Oh, some suits, sports jackets, shirts, shoes, and other clothing items—about half of those things aren't even in my closet now." He was still paying on clothes and shoes he had worn out!

We tend to be appalled at the size of the national debt. The fact is, the amount of personal debt in our nation is double the national debt. We aren't just a nation in debt...we are a nation of citizens who are in debt personally.

My foremost goal as I built my business was to get out of debt and then stay out of debt. I wanted to be free and clear. I can't tell you how great I felt when I finally reached that state. It was a great day when I received a statement from an oil company and it said, "Credit. Do not pay. $25.66." I realized that I had overpaid the last invoice and then I thought, "Well, if all else fails, I have a tank of gas coming!"

Do I use credit cards? Yes. It's prudent to do so for business records, especially as I travel internationally. But I have a policy of paying off those cards in full each month. I don't purchase beyond what I can afford to pay immediately when the invoice arrives in the mail.

I never encourage people to go into debt to expand their business. Rather, I encourage people to take the money they earn from retail or commercial sales to buy the product they need to expand their business. Use a portion of what you earn to increase your own earning power.

It Takes Money to Give Your Children an Extraordinary Life

As I observed the lifestyles of the professors at my college who had finished their doctorates and had been teaching ten to twenty years, I suddenly realized that they weren't significantly better off financially than I was as a teacher! The main difference I saw between myself and these professors was that their children now qualified for free tuition at the college where we taught. As far as I could tell, that was only going to perpetuate the cycle I described above for one more generation!

I didn't want my children to have just an average life. I wanted to be able to send them to the college of their choice—and pay cash for their tuition and expenses so they could graduate from college debt-free. I wanted to take them on trips and expose them to quality concerts, theatrical performances, and educational experiences that were a cut above. I wanted to be able to hire a helicopter so my son could observe whales in the waters off Hawaii—rather than write a paper on whales based on research from an encyclopedia. I wanted to be able to shop for school clothes with my daughter in San Francisco, rather than shop at the second-hand stores.

I'm not at all discounting the quality of parenting—love, faith, discipline, and values—that a poor parent can give to a child. I certainly was committed to giving my children those basic essentials. I just wanted to give them something beyond the basics.

It Takes Money to Live Well

You are more materialistic than you are probably willing to admit that you are.

It's always amazing to me that people who shop at the supermarket and the mall don't think of themselves as materialistic—they think they are just getting what they need...groceries, clothes, household items. In truth, we don't just purchase what we need in our nation, we purchase what we want.

For example, there are all kinds of foods you could buy to eat for breakfast. Many people want cereal for breakfast. There are all kinds of products that fall into the category of "cereal." Many people are very particular about the precise type and brand of cereal they want.

It doesn't take much to be clothed for sufficient warmth. But we all have very particular ideas about what kind of clothing we want to have, and some people are equally concerned about the brand of clothing they want to wear.

Even our most basic consumer choices have a great deal of want associated with them.

Furthermore, we want certain quantities of food. Some people want steak on weekends or a roast on Sunday. Some people want to spend more money on shoes than other people...there are those who want to take a vacation to the beach or to the mountains rather than stay at home on days off. The vast majority of purchases we make as consumers are rooted in what we choose...and what we choose is rooted in what we want.

I'm also never convinced when people tell me that they have no fantasies or daydreams about what they might want to own in the future. Many people are willing to admit that they want a home of their own, or that they want to remodel or upgrade their home in some way, or that they want a new home or a second vacation home. A materialistic person doesn't necessarily desire the most elaborate mansion on earth...but he does have a material desire for a particular kind of home.

The same goes for our cars, our desires for entertainment or recreation, our desires for travel or new experiences, and our desires for clothes and jewelry. We live in a material world and we have material concerns. We want a certain level of quality, style, and functionality in the material items we use and own.

There's a huge difference between materialism and greed. I do not at all advocate that a person should become greedy, which is an attitude rooted in power and an insatiable need for goods and services in order to achieve status.

To be materialistic does not mean that a person needs to be self-absorbed with the material world to the exclusion of being generous to others and especially to those in need. Some of the most generous people I know are also people who live high-quality lifestyles and enjoy "the finer things of life." They give away great sums of money—or in some cases, a great percentage of their income—and they take joy in what they can give. At the same time, they enjoy the luxuries they can afford and they have fun with their money.

Wealth and Greed are Very Different

Some of the wealthiest people I know also have these three traits:

- ❖ They are very hard workers. They don't stop working hard once they have acquired wealth. They continue to work hard—not only to continue to build their businesses but in efforts that benefit their particular community and the nation. They have a consistency in both their character and their work habits.
- ❖ They are very generous. Some of the best and the brightest stars in my particular organization have been incredibly generous to those who are under them in their organizations—in speaking at meetings on their behalf, in giving wise counsel, and in encouraging those who become discouraged. They are also incredibly generous to very worthy causes. I frankly don't know of anybody in my particular organization that I would call personally greedy. Every person who is a major success in my particular direct-sales business is a major giver to charitable causes. The causes differ widely, but that's one of the aspects I admire the most—nobody is a follower when it comes to how he or she gives. Every person is motivated by his or her own personal dream to see something changed in this world for the better.
- ❖ They are very modest about their achievements. I have a long-time friend who was my friend quite a while before I started my own business. I'd have popcorn and watch videos at his house with other friends. I knew what he did for a living but he never pressured me to become part of his organization—encourage, yes, but not heavy pressure. After I entered the business, I visited some of the people he had sponsored and helped through the years and I was amazed at the level of success he had achieved. I had no idea! That's true for

many of the people I know who have reached great heights in their business. They never brag about what they have done.

Greed is rooted in power. Greed is wanting everything you can put your hands on for your own status and consumption, regardless of who you may hurt in the process.

Wealth is simply having enough money to pay your bills, give your children an extraordinary life, and enjoy some of the luxuries of this world...and give to help others who are caught up in circumstances beyond their control to meet their basic needs and realize their dreams.

I'm in business to make money. To be in business for any other reason is to be just playing at business.

How You Spend Your Money is Up to You. But First You Need to Make Some. That's What it Means to be "In Business."

Chapter 5
You Don't Need a Business Degree, But You Do Need to Know Some Business Basics

When I first considered going into a direct-marketing business, I didn't know anything about business. I knew about music. I could play Beethoven sonatas all night long and sing songs hour after hour, but I had no idea about profit-and-loss statements.

I was amazed when I first heard this statement from Robert Kiyosaki: "OK, so that's your profession, but what do you do to make money work for you?" I had no idea what he meant! I thought a profession was what I did as WORK to make money. It had never dawned on me that I might find a way to have money work for me.

I actually knew very little about business.

Most network-marketing companies or franchise operations do not require that you have a specific degree or level of academic training. They don't require that you have a particular personality type, be of a particular age or race, be the citizen of a particular nation, or have a particular ethnic or cultural background.

What is required is a willingness to learn, a willingness to work, and a willingness to persevere. A cooperative attitude is a must.

Knowing some basics about business is to your advantage.

Get Smart About Money

One of the main reasons people fail in a self-owned business is because they are ignorant about money. They don't know how to balance a checkbook. They don't understand the enslavement of debt. They don't know the basic difference between credit and debit, liability and asset, accounts payable and accounts receivable.

I have met a number of women who have a cure for depression and discouragement: Shopping. They take one look at the stack of monthly bills they cannot pay, and they immediately go out to the mall and shop until they find a dress they just can't live without. For a few minutes in a dressing room they feel beautiful and successful so they purchase the dress—on credit—and bring it home. They have only added to their problem!

Turn your depression into a determination to get out of debt!

If you don't know how to manage money, learn how. Read books, attend seminars, and listen to tapes from people who have experience with money. Don't just listen to theory, and especially don't listen to theory from people who are broke. Find someone who has been successful in the management of their own personal finances and seek to discover what they did, when, and how.

Get Smart About Business Opportunities

I stated in an earlier chapter that I believe a network marketing business is one of the best opportunities in our nation today. Why? Because it doesn't take a lot of money to start up, it is the type of business many different types of people can do and succeed at doing, and success is determined primarily by effort, not innate talent or skills that take years to develop.

Not a Lot of Start-Up Capital

Most business ideas require a significant amount of start-up cash, sometimes fifty thousand dollars or more. That's a lot of venture capital to try to secure for a small-business enterprise.

Three things usually need to be in place before someone will be willing to invest venture capital in a new business idea:

1. The competition needs to be thoroughly and accurately evaluated. Great ideas are usually handed out to more than one person.
2. The timing of a new business start-up needs to be evaluated not only against the current marketplace, but the future marketplace. Many a good idea or product is

an old idea or product by the time it actually is manufactured and hits the marketplace.

3. Even if the idea is right and the timing is right, the management of the new venture had better be great. Most new businesses fail because they are improperly managed in the first six months of operation.

How does a consumables business stack up against this business wisdom?

Competitors

There are competitors, but a company with a track record that has survived because it has found benefits to the consumer—in price, quality, or service provided—is worth consideration.

Product in Marketplace

Many companies offer products that are considered mainstays in the marketplace. They offer products that people don't just want as a fad today, but rather, they offer products that people will want year after year—products that contribute to their health, their beauty, their management of time, or their quality of life.

Any person who is going to start a small business needs to do some research about the market, potential recruits, and product source. When I began my business, I chose a company with a product line of cleaning supplies, vitamins, and make-up. Today, I can market satellite dishes, telephone service, water purification systems, insurance, mortgage, and real-estate! I didn't change corporations—rather, the corporation expanded and diversified. Find a company that is growing.

Management

Most direct-sales companies have a built-in management plan. The most reputable companies don't just recruit a person to start a business—they help that person learn how to run their business in a successful way.

If you are considering a direct-sales company that doesn't fit these three criteria, think again. Fad products and singular-product companies rarely last. The more specialized the product, the more limited the customer base.

And finally, a direct-sales business can usually be started for just a few hundred dollars.

Year after year, surveys show:

- ❖ Eighty-five percent of America's millionaires own their own business or own a share of a privately owned business
- ❖ The biggest segment of millionaires fit this profile: Self-made entrepreneurs in their sixties
- ❖ Millionaires rarely are people who invent "better mousetraps." Rather, they tend to be people who have found ways to link existing ideas and technology in new ways

A direct-sales business offers these advantages: You don't have to wait until you are in your sixties to have amassed wealth, and most direct-sales companies are all about linking existing ideas, products, and technology in new ways.

A Diversity of Products and Services

What kind of business do you want to be in? Several years ago I read a book about self-owned businesses and the author indicated that before going into business, a person should answer these four questions:

- ❖ Do I want to sell products or services?
- ❖ Do I want to be in retail or wholesale?
- ❖ Do I want to work for a large company or a small company?
- ❖ Do I want to have a business primarily for the money...for the adventure and challenge...or for the personal recognition or satisfaction I might receive?

I laughed and said, "I want it all!"

The truth is, in my particular network-marketing business, I have it all. My business offers both products and services. In the offering of products, I'm on the wholesale side of things but in selling services, I function much more on the retail side of main street.

My personal business is technically a small business, but I'm embedded within a very large international corporation.

I'm into business for the money I make, the challenge of setting new goals, the adventures of travel as I build my own international business, and the personal satisfaction that I get from the money I can give away, the people I can influence to develop their potential, and the good fun I can have with my family and friends. Along the way I certainly have enjoyed the recognition from people I admire and respect.

Only you can answer what type of business you want to be in.

Minimal Risk

Virtually any small self-owned business has risk. The risk in a direct-sales business is very small, however. A direct-sales business requires the risk of some of your time, and usually a few hundred dollars. The organization with which I work has a money-back guarantee on its products so there is virtually no product liability.

I often say to those I'm attempting to recruit to the business...there's everything to gain and virtually nothing to lose. Even if you present products and a business plan to someone who says "no," that person may be someone from whom you can learn something interesting or with whom you find other common areas of your life that expand your network of people to call upon. Every encounter has a built-in reward for you if you are willing to look for it. I've had people say "no" to me who later said "yes." I've had people say "no" to me, but in the course of our conversation, I learned something interesting that helped me in my personal life or that helped me become a better business person. I've had people say "no" to me, but in the course of our association, they introduced me to other people who later said "yes" to me.

Did I enjoy having people say "no" to me? Of course not. But did I enjoy the encounters? Nine times out of ten, yes! I have learned to enjoy meeting people and getting to know people—people are fascinating and there's something to be gained from virtually every people encounter, even if that encounter is only a few minutes long.

How much money you invest in your own marketing company is up to you. Most companies do have a basic kit or set of products that are considered a basic investment. You also need to factor into your budget money for your own personal enrichment, motivation, and practical training. Many people I know set aside the first fifty to a hundred dollars they earn in a month to reinvest in their own personal enrichment. They use this money for educational and motivational tapes and books, and for traveling to and from seminars and meetings where they can hear special speakers or enjoy a time of fellowship with other people in their same business. The exact amount you set aside is up to you.

Finally, take a look at the pricing structure and reward system of the company you are considering. The good news about most network marketing businesses is that they increase their prices and rewards with inflation. In my particular business, prices and rewards are adjusted every three months against the economic price index. That means a person doesn't need to move more goods just to stay even. On most jobs, that isn't the case. People are asked to work harder and longer so they can continue to generate products that are behind the curve in pricing.

No Fixed Overhead Expenses

I never recommend that people get an office when they begin a network marketing business. Most people find they can conduct their business at the outset from a desk in the corner of their living room...a hide-away cabinet-style desk in their bedroom or extra bedroom...or even from the table in the formal dining room (assuming that table isn't used except for major holiday celebrations). A rolling two-drawer file cabinet or portable-file boxes can suffice. As you grow you may want to take your business out of the home—on the other hand, you may never want to leave home!

Set up a separate business checking account and you should have little trouble keeping your business separate from your personal expenditures—an important thing to have done come tax time.*

Be encouraged that there are very few licensing or regulatory laws governing direct-sales businesses. The usual record-keeping for tax purposes will suffice.

No Advertising or Warehousing Expenses

There are no advertising or upfront expenses required in the conducting of most network-marketing businesses. If you don't have an order for a product, don't buy it and store it! Wait until you have an order, then buy the product and immediately deliver it and require payment upon delivery.

No Payroll Expenses

One of the benefits of a direct-sales business is that you don't need to hire any employees if you don't want to. Most direct-sales organizations work on this principle: You find people you enjoy talking to and being around. Recruit them to the organization. They set up their own business. Because you recruited them to the organization, you reap some benefit from the business they generate. Therefore, it is to your benefit to encourage them in their business, train them, and do your best to help them become firmly established and off and running. The people you recruit to the organization, however, do not report to you in the traditional supervisory sense. You are not responsible for paying their salaries or any aspect of hiring, firing, promoting, or assigning work tasks to them. You work with those you recruit, but they don't work for you, and neither do you work for the person who recruited you.

One of the advantages of not having payroll expenses is a very practical one—no government forms to fill out and employer-related taxes and social security payments to file.

Another advantage of having no payroll is that you don't have the time intensive tasks of supervising, motivating, and

---

* At some point you may want to incorporate for the asset protection and tax reduction benefits. At the end of this book is information on an incorporation service I highly recommend. They are professional, affordable and offer a discount to the readers of this book.

evaluating staff performance. One of the most common complaints that employers have is that they spend lots of money paying employees for hours in which they don't do anything. One executive of an organization told me, "I have done some informal monitoring of some of the people under my supervision and have concluded that, on average, a person only truly works about twenty-five hours a week. The rest of the forty-hour week seems spent in trivial things that don't matter, and that don't truly generate income to the company...things like walking to and from the water cooler, talking extra unnecessary minutes on the phone, shuffling paperwork rather than 'dealing' with paperwork, and so forth. There are lots of wasted 'non-billable' hours."

"Isn't that discouraging?" I asked.

"Well," this executive laughed. " The good news is that when I look at other departments in our organization, I think the people I supervise are well above average. Some departments seem to get far fewer working hours a week per employee!"

In a direct-sales business, people don't earn from what they don't do. You don't need to spend a single minute in frustration over someone who is getting paid for doing little to no work.

The Profile of the Business I Want to Operate

When I took a look at all the advantages of a solely owned network marketing business, I saw a business that required:

- ❖ No major outlay of capital up front
- ❖ A quality line of products based upon solid product research and marketing research
- ❖ No advertising expenses
- ❖ No fixed overhead costs
- ❖ No warehousing expenses
- ❖ No personnel costs

I saw a business in which I was the sole owner...the sole decision-maker...the sole organizer and scheduler...and the sole reward receiver! I saw a business that provided a variety of goods and services that were of high quality.

I liked what I saw!

I Asked Myself, "What do I have to lose?"

The Answer Was, "Nothing!"

Chapter 6
Ride the Waves of Current Marketing Trends

Those who have studied market trends over time have noted that when our society was largely agricultural, people usually had to travel a significant distance to shop and a certain amount of commerce was conducted by peddlers, who went from farm to farm. The peddler had a wide variety of products on his cart, from cooking pots to bolts of fabric to farm and garden tools. I can remember a peddler who came by my grandmother's farm once a week. It was the highlight of the week for her and for us children who were visiting her. In the towns, one tended to find general stores, stores that were like much larger and more diverse peddler's carts. A general store had a smattering of just about everything a person could need or want.

Over time, the general stores broke up into specialty stores. Towns developed a main street that had a pharmacy, a grocery store, a hardware store, a clothing store, and so forth. Some of these specialty stores moved to the suburbs, generally in clusters called shopping centers. In time, the trend was for these specialty stores to be gathered together in one large air-conditioned and centrally heated building so that customers could move from store to store without braving the weather elements or moving their vehicles. We had entered the mall era.

Malls have become, in many cases, entertainment centers, so children can have fun in safety while parents shop to their heart's content.

And what is the current trend?

The focus is shifting back to the home. Rather than have families in which one person is the bread-winner and the other person is the bread-buyer, we now have families in which both spouses work. To save time, more and more purchases are being made from the home, with more and more products being shipped directly from warehouses to single-dwelling houses and apartments. The cost of the goods tends to be less, even with shipping and handling. Retail outlets are shrinking in size.

Some of the experts refer to this stay-at-home trend as "cocooning." They predict that people are going to do a lot more of their work at home rather than go into an office every day. Home-based businesses are going to increase in great numbers. People are also going to do a lot more of their comparison shopping and consumer purchasing from their homes, either via the Internet or by means of catalogs (including TV shopping channels) and phone calls.

Families are going to be "pulling in" and staying at home as families—watching videos or DVDs, or pursuing some other avenue of leisure entertainment. Family exercise rooms, teen rooms, or theaters in the home are becoming increasingly popular.

In many families, both parents work and children are booked into a steady stream of after-school activities. Time at home with family members has become an increasingly precious commodity. Those who are in their twenties and thirties these days value the acquisition of possessions, but just as much, they value having free time to pursue their own interests, ideas, and the relationships they value.

I recently heard about a man who is in his early forties. He has risen to be the president of a company and makes more than $200,000 a year. He is giving up that job to take a position that pays about half that much. Why? Because his higher-paying job takes him out of town four days a week. The lower-paying job will allow him to be at home every night. This man awoke one morning and realized that two of his children were in high school and one was in junior high. He was running out of time to be with his children—only a few years were left before the kids left home for college. He wanted to make the most of those years.

A marketing executive for one of the largest chain department stores told me not long ago that according to their marketing study projections, within ten years, people will be purchasing the majority of their goods and services over the

Internet and having them delivered directly to their homes...in some cases, they will be saving money, and in other cases, they will only be saving time. Time, however, is money to most people. And, as one shopper pointed out to me, when you stay out of the malls, you aren't subject to impulse buying. In her case, and no doubt in the case of many others like her, just staying out of the malls saves her money even if an individual item she orders on her computer is a little more expensive by the time it is delivered!

If you happen to have a direct-sales business in which the consumer saves money and saves time...that's a double bonus!

Many department stores are now offering things we never dreamed would be associated with department stores—from life insurance to airline and cruise tickets to real-estate products. Projections call for a number of major department store chains to be totally on-line in the next decade.

Look for a direct-sales business that is up on these trends!

Four Additional Marketing Trends

In addition to the trend back to the home, here are four additional marketing trends in our society:

Trend 1: Fast and Easy

Time and convenience are the currency of our age. If a person has a choice between paying twenty cents more for a gallon of milk and spending ten extra minutes getting that milk, I guarantee you the person is going to spend a little more to save a little time. That person will pop into a quick-stop store of some kind and pay fifteen to twenty percent more on average just to save the long walk and long lines in the mega discount store with the huge parking lot.

In the next ten years, one out of four Americans will be at least sixty years old. What do more mature people want? Service! They don't want hassle or delay.

In your direct-sales business, two of the most important words you can adopt as a mind set for the service you deliver are these: Fast and Easy. Be the person who delivers product right now, without any excuses or delay.

Trust me, I'm just this kind of fast and easy consumer the experts are talking about!

I recently invited a friend to come up to my home at Lake Tahoe for a week. I had known this woman for about twenty-five years and we had a great time together—just talking, relaxing, reading by the fireplace, enjoying the view of the lake.

One evening I suggested we watch one of my favorite videos. In that home, my very technical and video-savvy son has set up an entertainment system that is just amazing. I couldn't for the life of me figure out how to work the videotape player.

The more frustrated I became at not being able to figure out which buttons to push, the more determined I became that we were going to watch my movie of choice that evening. I finally put on my coat, drove down to the nearest store that sold electronic equipment, and said, "Do you have a television set with a built-in videotape player—something that has just one or two buttons to push that I can plug in immediately?"

They did.

So for about $350, my friend and I watched the movie I wanted to see that evening!

When my son comes up to visit, he can figure out all the buttons on all the remote control units associated with our fancy entertainment system. As for me, give me something with two buttons that is virtually foolproof and that requires virtually no figuring out.

I want it fast and easy...even if I have to pay more!

Trend 2: Good Value for the Dollar

Everybody wants a deal. That doesn't mean everybody wants cheap merchandise. People are willing to pay for quality—they just want good value for the dollar.

Find a company that goes the second mile in producing a line of products that is truly excellent. Check into the company's research and development department. Try the products for yourself. Make sure the products work...that good solid research has gone into their development and improvement over the years...and that the marketing plan and pricing offered by the company represent a genuinely good deal for the purchaser.

Don't give away your services or your products. There may be rare exceptions to this, but as a general principle, place a value on what you offer. You may very well be sending a signal that your services or products aren't worth much if you give away too much for free.

If you go to a plastic surgeon and he says to you, "I'll do this surgery for $29.95," you wouldn't be able to get out that office fast enough. If a dentist told you, "I'll do this procedure for free," you'd probably be highly suspect. You would likely interpret "free" as being "experimental," as in, "he's never done this before and I'm the first person he's trying this on!"

Trend 3: A Piece of the Action

People today want every piece of the economic pie they can get. That's the driving force behind all businesses that have commissions, royalties, profit-sharing, or residuals as part of their structure.

Most people are willing to work a little harder up front if they know there's a piece of the action coming back to them down the line, and especially if there's a renewable piece of the action coming back to them repeatedly through the years. People who receive a commission or a rebate, refund, percentage-of-profit payment or whatever other term you may want to call cash associated with every purchase and every sale...are people who tend to work harder, work longer, and work happier.

There's a story about three traveling salesman who got caught in a snowstorm in Montana. They were holed up in a little motel for several days. One morning they were sitting in the motel's café wondering just when they might be able to get back on the road. Suddenly, a man came roaring up to the café entrance in a four-wheel-drive truck. He got out and came into the café and sat down at the counter.

The three traveling salesmen rushed over to him and said, "Hey, can we get out of here?"

He stirred his coffee slowly and slowly drawled, "That all depends?"

"Depends on what?" they asked.

"Depends on whether you're on salary or commission."

Wouldn't you like to get just a little portion of every phone card your friends purchase? Or a little portion of the price of an airline ticket they purchase? Or a little portion of the price of pre-paid or insurance premiums?

Trend 4: More Reliance on Word of Mouth

Which movies do you see? Which restaurants are you eager to try out? Which products do you rush out to purchase? Which investments trigger a call to your stock broker? In all likelihood, each of these questions can be answered, "The one my friend, associate, colleague, or even the stranger in the elevator told me about!" We seem to be listening to other "common folk" more than to so-called expert critics.

We all give other people free advice! But when was the last time a department store or supermarket gave you a check because you recommended to a friend to go to that store to shop? A direct-sales business puts you in line for the very same customers, with quality products, and an opportunity for a check to show up in your mail!

How Do These Trends Relate to a Network Marketing Business?

Consider for a moment that every person is a consumer. The professional consumer buys product for himself directly as a wholesaler and keeps the traditional retail mark-up for himself. The amateur consumer pays retail and gives away the profit to a local store.

The very first line of profit for every direct-sales person I know is this: Become a professional consumer. Find a company that has products you like, use regularly, and intend to keep on using. Become a user-distributor, or in other words, a professional consumer. Even if you don't see any cash flow into your wallet, you will experience significant savings on your selected items that you are already purchasing as an amateur consumer at the local supermarket or mall.

The next step in network marketing is to tell your friends, acquaintances—and the friends and acquaintances of your friends and acquaintances—about the products you are using and selling. Begin to network with other people. As I began my business, I simply told other people about the products I was using and invited them to try the products for themselves and become professional consumers who could enjoy the same great savings I was enjoying. When people became professional consumers, I encourage them to tell their friends and pass on the good news.

Not only did I offer fabulous products and great prices to my individual customers, I also made it possible for them to receive these products at their door, which meant that they not only saved money, but the time and energy shopping for the products.

In addition to individual customers, I found some businesses that could routinely use some of the products I offered—at good savings to them and with excellent results—and I set up some commercial accounts that were serviced directly by my company.

The purchases by other individual customers and commercial customers gave me some cash flow. In essence, I got a little piece of every purchase they made.

Every year in the music-teaching career I purchased music from publishers, who in turn paid a royalty to the composers and lyricists. I was always fascinated by the idea that a person could produce a product once and continue to receive a certain amount of reward from that effort for many years into the future.

My direct-sales business gave me that same opportunity. I made a sale once to a commercial account and month after month as that commercial account reordered (an automatic process set up with my corporate headquarters), I still received residual benefit from the purchase. No new time or effort was required on my part—only a periodic call or visit to update their order.

Once I began to experience some positive cash flow into my business—and my personal bills were being paid—I made a concerted effort to recruit as many other professional consumers as I could recruit. I encouraged each of them to build a wholesale distribution network similar to what I had built.

I didn't limit myself to the immediate area in which I lived. I helped people set up a similar system of professional consumerism all over nation, pretty much following leads wherever they took me.

J. Paul Getty once said, "I'd rather have one percent of a hundred men's productivity, than to have a hundred percent of my own productivity." That's the principle at the heart of the business I entered. I just chose to take his statement a step further. I'd rather have a small percent of a thousand people's productivity or purchases—or ten thousand people's productivity or purchases—than one hundred percent of my own productivity. I can only do so much in a day. But reaping a very small part of what many other people are doing...that's where the cash truly begins to accumulate.

The concept is very simple...very basic...and can be very lucrative.

A network marketing business is totally in sync with current marketing trends. Catch the wave!

Play Keep-Away Instead of Give-Away When It Comes to the Profit Margin.

Chapter 7
The More You Know About the Products You Are Selling, the Easer it is to Sell Them

Audiences around the world have heard me say repeatedly:

- ❖ Use the products.
- ❖ Love the products.
- ❖ Know the products.
- ❖ Use the products.
- ❖ Love the products.
- ❖ Experience the products.

There's no better testimony to the value and quality of the products that you are selling than the statement, "I use this and love it!" Some time ago, a man who works with me told me that he had sold our dietary food bars to a man who saw him eating one, asked about it, and ended up purchasing some because he wanted to lose some weight. He ended up becoming a major distributor for the food bars to others. My colleague said, "What if I hadn't been eating that bar!"

When I was growing up, I lived with my Aunt Ethel and Uncle Raymond. There were four of us kids in her house—my two cousins, and my sister and I. We heard that there was a prize at the bottom of every Wheaties cereal box and we children decided we wanted those prizes!

Uncle Raymond thought we should eat one box of Wheaties and the prize in the bottom would go to one of us...then we'd eat another box of Wheaties and the prize would go to another of us...and so forth until we had finished four boxes of cereal. That wasn't at all what we children had in mind. We each wanted our own box of Wheaties!

We convinced Uncle Raymond that we would eat cereal for breakfast, morning snack, afternoon snack, and anytime we were allowed to eat cereal. Uncle Raymond relented and allowed us to each have our own very large box of Wheaties...with one rule: We could not reach down the side of the box and get the prize at the bottom. We had to eat our way to the bottom of the box.

Over the next couple of weeks, we children ate Wheaties as if it was candy. We loved Wheaties. Why? Because every bowl of Wheaties we ate brought us a little closer to our goal of the prize at the bottom of the box.

Use all the products you are selling. Know from your own experience how well they work. You'll not only have greater credibility with your customers, but you'll also gain new insights into the best selling points of the product. Grow to love the product you are selling.

Information and Understanding are Two Different Things

One of our clients is a very accomplished cyclist. What makes him amazing to me is that he has no legs—he lost them in the Vietnam War. He wears artificial limbs.

One day this man went into a gym, fully clothed, and he saw one of the physical therapists being what he considered to be quite harsh and impatient as he was working with a young man who had no legs. The cyclist said to him, "Hey man, lighten up a little bit. You could make this more enjoyable."

The therapist replied gruffly, "What do you know about it? You're not a trained therapist."

"No," the cyclist replied. Then, as he pulled up the legs of his trousers to reveal his artificial legs, he added, "But I understand."

There's a lot to be said for understanding that comes from experience, rather than more formal instruction. There's a lot to be said for having the right information—which sometimes comes only from formal instruction. Seek both.

The only way to get true understanding about a product is to use it and to have experience with it. There's also no better way to learn the major selling points of a product than to use the product regularly.

What You Like About a Product is What Will Sell the Product to Others

When I first began my business, I thought some of the products were fairly high in price. Then I learned more about the products and I was amazed at what I learned.

First, the product I was selling was a concentrate. My one little bottle of product was equal to five large jugs of a competitor's product. The competitor's product had mostly water in it. I didn't find it difficult at all to add water to my concentrate and fill up a squirt bottle I could reuse a number of time.

I began to do the math. Five large jugs of the competitor's product were significantly more expensive than my one little bottle of concentrate and my reusable plastic container. The product I was selling wasn't more expensive as I thought—it was significantly less expensive!

I learned more. Since my bottle of concentrate was delivered to me along with a number of other items, I needed to factor in both the gasoline money and time I saved by not making four additional trips to the store to purchase the competitor's products. In calculating the time, I figured I saved at last twelve minutes of shopping time each trip to the store. (In the store where I had shopped, the items such as my concentrate were halfway across a warehouse-sized room, so shopping time and check-out times were significant!)

It was also pointed out to me that not only was I paying for large plastic jugs that I wasn't reusing, but as a taxpayer I was paying for the trash pick-up and disposal of those plastic jugs. I was paying for the landfill they required! And in the end, I was paying for the environmental damage caused by some of the chemicals used in the manufacturing of the plastic containers.

In recent years, I've taken a number of cruises and I have always felt sick as the ship crossed through waters where various currents converged. It was like crossing an open sewage line with all kinds of trash floating in the water, many of them plastic containers of various sizes. And to think that many of those containers had held product that was eighty to ninety percent water! It was all I could do to keep from giving my concentrate-is-better-for-us-all speech to anybody who would listen!

The more information I learned about my bottle of concentrate, the more cost effective that bottle of concentrate began to look.

Then I realized that if I could get just twenty people to order the concentrate on a regular basis through me—repeat orders over time—my bottle of concentrate wouldn't cost me anything. I'd more than be compensated for its cost through the residual amount I received from my customers.

Free concentrate was the best price I could imagine!

Now this concentrate was for a type of product that I used regularly in significant amounts. Not having this expense just meant more cash freed up in the family budget for other items.

Given accurate and complete information, I felt fully ready to present the product to potential customers, and to encourage those customers to recruit their own set of customers, who might recruit their own set of customers.

I wasn't trying to sell something to a person that wasn't a product they already needed and used regularly.

I was selling people on the idea of using a product they already used and saving a great deal of money in the process! I was selling people a superior product that helped the environment!

Get fully informed about the product you are selling.

Embedded within the information you acquire will be the inspiration you need to sell your product with enthusiasm.

The Best Teacher is Experience.

PART III

Positive Commitment

Chapter 8
Oh, But You ARE a Salesperson!

I remember telling my mother as a young woman, "I'll never be able to sell anything like you do." There was a little pride mingled in with that lament. After all, I was a musician and I was glad to be a musician. Musicians didn't have anything to do with sales!

Then one day I was standing in front of a five-hundred-voice choir of young people in the Pasadena, California convention center, and I realized, "I'm standing here selling Bach! I'm selling these kids on good music. I'm selling them on the idea of singing the music of a classical composer, and doing so from the depths of their being, all the way to their toenails."

Regardless of what line of work you think you are gifted to do, there's an element of selling in that line of work. To some degree, you sold your employer on your ability to do the job at the time you were hired! You continue to sell your employer on your abilities and the reason you deserve a promotion or a raise. To some degree, you are selling your clients, customers, patients, students, parishioners, or patrons on the service, beliefs, and products you provide or espouse. As a parent, you are selling your children on the idea of displaying good behavior, including good manners and good school performance. Every person has a degree of selling in his or her life, even if it's just part of trying to win or keep someone's admiration, respect, or affection. We might call it putting our best foot forward, being on our best behavior, or winning friends and influencing people. If you are trying to convince anybody to do, think, or believe something...you are selling.

Plain and simple, you have more sales ability than you think you have!

Seven Facets of Good Salesmanship

Salesmanship in a network marketing business has at least seven basic facets:

1. <u>Make the Calls</u>. Making calls and setting up appointments—either to sell product or present a business plan—is at the foundation of all network marketing salesmanship. There's no substitute for making calls!

   Set a quota for yourself when it comes to calls. I once heard about an investments broker who told himself that he was going to make a hundred calls a day...and he did it! That's an incredibly high number. Most people in network marketing can, however, make ten to fifteen calls a day, and out of that number, most will get at least two or three appointments—sometimes a higher number.

   In the comic strips, Charley Brown once noted, "Life is a lot like an ice cream cone—you have to lick it one day at a time."

   Countless people live outside the moment. They stare into the past with nostalgia or regret. They gaze into the future with longing or sometimes fear. They do not truly relish, seize, or fully experience the moment called RIGHT NOW.

   It's especially important that you not procrastinate or put off the setting of appointments or sales calls. That's the one area of your business where it is absolutely vital that you seize the moment every day.

   Make a pact with yourself that tonight you are going to get on the phone and make your appointments for this week. Make a decision about whom you are going to contact about retail sales.

   The most successful people I know are those who keep themselves tightly scheduled—they continually are working to set up meetings so they might present their plans or products.

   Be diligent in making calls and appointments. It's the core of the work that you do. Keep at it...keep at it...keep at it.

A number of years ago a man met Gary Player, the internationally famous golfer, and said, "I'd give anything if I could hit a golf ball the way you do."

Mr. Player very thoughtfully replied to him, "No, you wouldn't. You would if it was easy, but it isn't easy to hit a golf ball like I do. To hit a golf ball like I do, you have to get up every morning at five o'clock and go out to the driving range and hit a thousand balls. When your hand starts to bleed, you go into the clubhouse and bandage it up, and then you go back out and hit another thousand balls. Now, do you really want to hit a golf ball like I do?"

People have said to me through the years, "Beverly, I'd give anything to be as successful as you are in your business."

My response? "Would you really give anything? Would you really give the effort, the time, the commitment, the intensity?"

Many times when it comes to the work related to success, people back off. They want the rewards of success, but not the work that results in success.

How many phone calls did you really make last week?

How many times did you really show your plan or make a presentation last month?

2. <u>Keep Your Contact List Active.</u> Directly related to your calls is your contact list. Whether it's for retail or for distributors, keep your contact list current. Always have a next prospect in mind. Always be working on new appointments.

Just recently I pulled into a gas station and the attendant said, "This is the fourth time you've been in here this week. What do you do to put so many miles on your car?"

I told him I had a direct-sales business and asked, "Have you ever used our products?" He said, "I used to use them. I loved them."

I said, "How much do you want of what, and when do you want it delivered?" I had a new customer in the time it took this man to fill up my tank and check my oil.

3. Learn to memorize names. Write down names in your journal so the next time you encounter a particular group of people, you can refresh your memory and walk into the group able to speak to people by name.

   Don't give in to the thinking, "I just can't remember names but I never forget a face." People want to hear you call them by name. You can memorize names if you put your mind to it.

4. Get Some Cash Flowing. The fastest way I know to get cash flowing into your business is to acquire one or more commercial accounts. Put your initial focus on getting an account or two that will order month after month after month. In most direct-sales businesses, you won't even have to deal with the paperwork related to that account down the line—the corporate headquarters likely will handle that for you.

   My basic formula for priming the cash pump in network marketing is this:

   Find yourself twelve to fifteen good customers. A good customer is someone who orders repeatedly and pays with checks that don't bounce.

   You won't get rich on these twelve to fifteen good customers, but you will generate a little extra cash flow into your life. Use your cash to invest in personal development materials.

   If at all possible, try to have three of these good customers be commercial accounts—small businesses or large businesses that use the products you offer and order repeatedly.

   Then, set a goal for yourself of building a network of people who each can find twelve to fifteen good customers. Move out of the comfort zone of your own friends and club members. Talk to your neighbors about what you do and how good it feels to have a little extra money every month from good customers. Encourage them to try the products and then recruit their own set of customers. Eventually, of course, as they develop a set of good customers, they are going to be much more interested in trying to recruit new people who can network with people totally unknown to you.

Very quickly, the results begin to compound in most network-marketing businesses. Within a couple of years of steady effort, a person can build a business that produces a fairly steady second income. Such income is not only good to have in paying bills and building a retirement fund, but it is also fun to give to special causes.

5. <u>Know and Use the Tools You Have Been Given.</u> My father helped build houses in the time when he wasn't working as an immigrations officer. We children would help him after school. Now, we weren't allowed to wear a tool belt and do any of the real construction work, but we certainly were good at picking up small pieces of scrap lumber and the nails and other trash that always seems to emerge at a construction site. I always admired those men who were able to wear a tool belt with all of the various tools hanging on it and the pockets filled with the basics of the trade.

Know your tools! As you listen to a particular training tape or motivational tape, make notes. Know the materials you are passing on to others. Become conversant about all aspects of your business, including the promotional materials.

Tools are meant to be used. That's their function—at a construction site and in network marketing. Those who use the tools, as opposed to letting them gather dust in the corner of the bedroom or become buried in the trunk of the car, are people who are on their way to building a business.

So many people ignore the tools made available to them. Some do this out of ignorance—they haven't fully explored the tools for themselves and they don't know the value of what they have in their possession. Others fail to use the tools out of arrogance—they think they know how to sell better than the hundreds of people who have gone before them and risen to the top of their enterprise.

I've encountered a number of people through the years who have told me, "Listen, I'm a top salesman where I work now. I know how to sell. In fact, I have been told I could sell ice to an Eskimo. I don't need to follow any particular system. I know what works for me."

Invariably, the person who makes that statement does one of two things—he or she comes around to using and relying on the tools they have been given because they come to see the great value of the tried-and-proven methods contained in them...or they muddle along using their own system until they fail or become highly frustrated and discouraged.

6. Read Business Periodicals. Keep up with current trends. I find the *USA Today* business section particularly informative. It's written in easy-to-read and easy-to-understand language. I also read the *Wall Street Journal* and watch for special magazine articles related to business and marketing trends.

7. Stay up with technology. I recently read this quip: "The day after you buy a computer, it is obsolete. But if you don't buy a computer, you'll be obsolete." Maintain a positive attitude toward new technology. It has the potential to make your life easier and your productivity higher.

As a child I spent part of a number of summers at my aunt's house on her farm in Kansas. I always thought it was great fun to visit the farm. We'd catch frogs and horned toads, bother the cows, and ride the horses. In her big old farm house my aunt had a phone that hung on a wall in her kitchen. She'd go to it occasionally, pick up the receiver, wind the crank on the side of the phone, and then holler into receiver, "Hello, Central? Ring up Ma down the road for me!"

Later, she had a phone that she didn't have to ring up to get the central operator. She could just speak into it and say, "Hello, Operator, I'd like to talk to the Smiths over on 24th Street."

Still later, there was the rotary phone. If your finger didn't fit in the holes of the dial, you could always use a pencil. How amazing it was to us when we got a phone that had push buttons for the numbers—and how much lighter that plastic-encased phone was than the old metal-cased rotary phone.

Do you remember the first cellular phone? They were like carrying around a brick. You could get a headache just carrying one around up to your ear for a half hour.

Cellular phones got smaller and smaller, and in some places now, all I see are ear pieces connected with a thin wire to a mouthpiece, with a receiver attached at the person's belt.

The most amazing innovation about the phone, however, was not in how the phone itself changed, but rather, what and who the phone could link us to. The day we all plugged our phones into the Internet and began to send e-mail, our lives changed fundamentally even if we weren't aware of the change. And now, that technology is wireless.

Technologies are merging, and at the same time expanding. Cellular phones have greater and greater ranges internationally. Hand-held PDA's can include phone and e-mail functions. Television sets and computer screens have become one and the same. Who knows where we'll go next!

Most of us have wondered in the past, "How will I ever learn to use this?" But we did. In just the past twenty years, we've learned how to use cell phones, the laptop computer, the videotape player (and DVD player), deal with e-mail, order items on-line, and schedule our lives electronically rather than in an appointment book filled with pen and paper.

Ordinary people can learn to do extraordinary things...if they are only willing to make the effort.

Keep Sight of the Big Picture

Don't get bogged down in details or minutia. Keep the big picture in mind. Good salesmanship is not by rote—it's as much art as science.

When I was nine years old, I finally was allowed to take piano lessons. Prior to that time, I had enjoyed the sound of the piano. I enjoyed messing around on the keyboard. But I had no concept of musical notes or how the little black marks on a piece of paper might translate into music from a piano.

My mother had a piece of sheet music that she enjoyed playing. It was titled "Far Away Places." I grew up knowing those lyrics that seem so appropriate to my life now: "Those far away places with strange-sounding names are calling, calling to me." I could play bits and pieces of that song by picking out the right-sounding notes on the piano, and I could sing a few lyrics to go with them from memory. But I couldn't play the entire song the way my mother did, and I made no connection between the sheet music and the black and white keys on the piano.

During my first piano lesson, the teacher explained to me the lines and spaces on a staff of music, and she taught me the names of the notes. She opened up a whole new world to me! I suddenly connected the sound of the notes on the piano with the look of the notes on a piece of paper. Wow! I quickly saw that if I could read music, I could play on the piano anything I could read!

Some people in their business life are just picking out a technique or using a measure or two of a method. They don't really have a grasp of the big picture—they don't see how things fit together.

Take everything that is given to you by the experts in your field—the basic concepts, the key principles, the steps required, the tried-and-true methods—and seek to put them together into a whole.

Your calling discipline...contact list...knowledge of trends...memory skills...use of technology...and use of the information and sales tools you have been given...work together as a whole. Just one aspect of salesmanship isn't going to reap big results—putting all aspects of good salesmanship into effect will result in high productivity.

Do Everything You Do With Diligence and Excellence

Choose to become a person who is committed to the pursuit of excellence and to living a disciplined, diligent, dedicated business life.

One of the most highly prized possessions in high school was my school sweater. My mother had told me that she thought this sweater was an extra that I really didn't need, and she made it clear that if I wanted a school sweater, I'd have to earn it myself.

So I did.

I got fifty cents for every evening that I worked as a baby-sitter. I saved every fifty cents I earned until the day I had the twelve dollars that it cost to buy a school sweater. That sweater cost me twenty-four evenings of my life. It was very valuable to me because I had earned it myself!

I had already earned various letters and emblems in high school and I can't tell you how good I felt as I sat and stitched those letters and emblems onto my new sweater. That sweater was a wonderful symbol of achievement to me—I had studied and excelled in various areas to earn the letters and I had worked hard to earn the sweater. Let me assure you, excellence in what you do plus hard work is always a winning combination.

Never Stop Selling

Part of the diligence and dedication associated with salesmanship is this simple principle: Never stop selling. Always seek to grow your business.

My first check from a network marketing company was $9.57. Today I earn in six figures annually...and all projections say that will continue for the rest of my life. I feel truly blessed. But I also know that I worked hard to get from that first check to the last check. And, I haven't stopped trying to expand my business. I'm still actively recruiting new people to the business, still speaking at inspirational meetings, still servicing customers, and still having both phone and face-to-face appointments with people to encourage their growth and help give them practical advice.

If You Want ALL Your Dreams To Come True, Don't Oversleep and Don't Quit.

Chapter 9
Practice Makes Perfect... Growth!

Years ago when I taught piano lessons privately I'd have children come to me with great ambition to be an accomplished pianist. I'd say to them, "Do you want to play like this?" and I'd launch into a fast, showy, intricate piece.

They'd say, "Yeah, that's the way I want to play!"

I'd then say, "Well, here's how you can play like that. Here's what you have to do this week if you really want to play like that."

I'd play a little scale of just a few notes that was played with one hand.

They'd frown. "No, that's not the way I want to play. That's too boring." I'd say, "Oh, you want to play like this..." and I'd launch again into a fancy piece with lots of runs and trills."

"Yeah," they'd reply enthusiastically. "That's the way I want to play."

"Before you can play like that, you have to play like this," and I'd repeat the little scale. "And, if you practice that all week and are good at it by the time you come for your next lesson, I'll let you practice a little scale with your other hand the next week."

Some left discouraged. They quickly gave up. Playing the piano the way they wanted to play the piano was too hard and it seemed to take too long. They never became pianists.

The students who were willing to play the scales, however—and to practice week in and week out with diligence—were the ones who learned to play, and some of them, to play very well.

The same is true for your business, of course.

- ❖ Listen to a tape every day that pertains to your business
- ❖ Read a part of a book every day
- ❖ Make calls every day
- ❖ Make presentations every week

❖ Go to the seminars available to you to improve your skills

❖ It's in the basics that you develop your business

One thing I know about great pianists—they still practice by playing simple scales! In fact, one of the greatest pianists of all time once said that if he didn't play an hour's worth of scales every day, he could tell it in his next performance. And, he said, if he didn't play an hour's worth of scales every day over the time he presented two performances, the critics could tell it. If he didn't play an hour's worth of scales every day for the time encompassed by three performances, the audience knew it!

Success Isn't Instant

I'm not a patient person. I want instant hair, instant eyelashes, instant diet success, instant food out of a microwave. A very high percentage of women I know also want instant lives, including instant marriages, instant careers, and instant success. We'd trade in the nine months of pregnancy on nine days of nursery decorating if we could.

Life isn't an instant process, however, especially when it comes to success.

Although the rewards can be tremendous in a direct-sales business, and good rewards can be realized in a relatively short period of time, there isn't any such thing as an overnight success in direct sales—or, for that matter, in any area of life I know about other than winning a lottery or sweepstakes. Even then, the success if often short-lived and narrowly focused because the winner isn't prepared to handle the amount of money that comes his or her way.

Rather, the success in direct sales is nearly always a slow, steady rise that eventually arcs upward into what it known as a geometric curve. The harder a person works the faster that rise occurs and the sooner a person gets to the "geometric curve" part!

A Geometric Curve

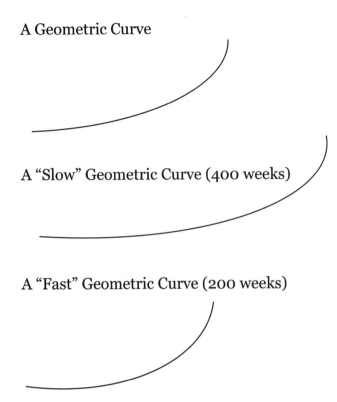

A "Slow" Geometric Curve (400 weeks)

A "Fast" Geometric Curve (200 weeks)

You'll notice in each of these diagrams that the curve is the same. It's the time frame that's different!

At the outset, set your mind toward the idea of slow, steady progress and the need for you to persevere. Don't allow yourself to get hyped up and overly excited. You'll be setting yourself up for a fall. And, don't allow yourself to become overly discouraged. You'll quit.

Decide how many hours you can, or are willing to, devote to your direct-sales business...and then devote those hours to your business. Don't feel guilty for not working more hours. Don't work fewer hours. Set aside blocks of time that you are going to devote to your business and then work hard in those hours.

I have business associates in eastern Europe who have made a commitment to showing their direct-marketing business plan to at least three prospective clients a day. Three plans in a day.

They're determined to do this for two years.

That's an ambitious goal. Many people think they're doing well if they make three presentations in a week...or even a month.

Now, you do the math.

If you're presenting three times a DAY, six days a week, that's going to be more than seventy times a month.

If even one in every seven people buys into the plan, that's going to be ten sales or ten recruits a month.

The person who is showing the plan only three times a month, with one in seven people buying into the plan, is going to take an average of two years to accumulate that same number of sales or recruits!

Whose business is going to take off like a rocket? Whose business is going to stagnate?

Which person is going to be highly motivated by his or her own results and success? Which person is likely to become discouraged at not seeing much growth?

"But," you may be saying to yourself, "to find three people a day who are willing to hear a presentation, I'd probably need to make several dozen calls."

Yes. Those European colleagues are doing just that. They are devoting themselves to four or five hours a day of virtually nonstop phone work in order to set up three appointments a day. They spend another hour or two calling to educate, inspire and motivate people they've already recruited. In all, they are working twelve to fourteen hours a day. Being European, of course, their appointments are generally associated in some way with eating, so work-time and meal-time tend to blend together.

I teased one of my associates that he was "dining his way to the top." He smiled and said, "What a way to get there!"

Again, do the math. A person who is presenting three times a day, six days a week for two years—at the rate of only one in seven successes—is going to have 240 recruits or sales at the presentations a day...wow, the growth is nearly exponential, or as a young friend of mine says, "Off the chart to the point you're in orbit!"

Ask yourself: If you maintain your current level of effort and productivity, where will you be in your business by this time next year? Two years from now? Three years from now?

The Man Who Rolls Up His Sleeves Seldom Loses His Shirt.

Chapter 10
Sidestep the Ridicule With a Smile and a Provocative Question

Every business I know has an opposition of some kind. Sometimes the opposition takes the form of a competitor. Sometimes a rival. Sometimes a critic. And sometimes...a jealous or mean-spirited person who just likes to needle you!

In the early days of my business I received a great deal of teasing from my colleagues. I still don't know if they meant to be cruel or if they were just trying to communicate, but I know that if I had allowed myself to internalize their comments, I would have been hurt. Everything about what they said to me was in some way demeaning, critical, or a put down. In essence, they didn't want me to succeed. They especially didn't want me to succeed at something they didn't understand or couldn't do.

How can you deflect critical comments without internalizing them?

My best advice is to agree with your critics, and do so with a smile. If they call you a name, fire right back, "You're right! That's who I am and who I'm going to be, all the way to the top!" Or, "Yeah, can you believe it? I'm having a blast at this!" Or, "I've got the greatest opportunity in the world!"

If a co-worker criticizes you for working so hard on weekends or in the evening, just smile and say, "I've got an exit strategy from this dead-end, low-ceiling job...do you?" Or, "How is your retirement plan coming along these days?"

You don't have to say another word.

If a person says to you in a teasing, derogatory way, "How was that big weekend seminar you were planning to attend?" Reply, "It was one of the best times I've had in a very long time!"

Always reply with a smile—a smile that says, "Say what you want, I know something that you don't know!"

I learned that if people see you are happy, they either think you aren't informed—that you're a little dim-witted or unintelligent—or that you truly are informed and that you know something they don't know! Either way, you win!

If you run from the comments, try to ignore the comments, or respond with a defense comment, the other person gets a certain amount of satisfaction. If you respond with a smile and a light-hearted positive statement, the other person is defused and you walk away from the encounter without any internalizing of their words or attitude.

If you present your business to a person and they say "no" to you, you can expect that person to be a little negative or critical the next time you see him. He's likely to say, "How's that business of yours going?"—and they usually say it with a smirk as if to say, "I'm telling you, you're in a losing proposition and I'm the smart one for staying out of it." Just smile right back and say, "It's going great! How's your job going? Have you received a bonus check this week?"

If people ask you how much money you are making or how long you've been in business and how much you've earned during that time...smile and say, "I'm right on track." You don't owe people an answer. It's none of their business! If you answer a personal question that you are uncomfortable answering, you'll open yourself up to a lot more questions from that person and end up feeling even more uncomfortable!

I remember one person who made this comment to me the first time I drove up to a dean's meeting in the days when I was still a faculty member by day and a business person by night. My car at the time was my first Cadillac, and I must admit, I took a little pleasure in parking my car in a fairly obvious place among the Fords, VWs, and little Toyotas driven by the other faculty members. This man said in a very snide tone of voice, "Well, they certainly are paying their faculty a lot these days."

I turned and said, "They aren't paying me enough as a faculty member to keep gasoline in that car. My real income comes in from another source."

That kept him guessing!

The Power of a Positive Question

Through the years, I heard all kinds of criticism and snide remarks as I grew my business. I also became very good at responding to some of those critics! I discovered it is very good to respond to a critical comment with a positive question. For example...

Critic: "Well, what did you do this weekend? Betcha went to one of this motivational week-ends, didn't you?"

Me: "Sure did. How's your retirement plan coming along?

Critic: "All that direct-sales stuff is just a lot of hype."

Me: "Have you been to a football game lately? And by the way, how much did your salary increase last year?"

Critic: "Those direct-sales people are a bunch of kooks."

Me: "When was the last time you spent a week at an island resort and laughed until your sides ached?"

The Strength of Returning an Insult With a Compliment

If a person fires an insult at you, fire a smile back at that person along with a positive compliment!

"You look nice today..."

"I like what you had to say at the meeting yesterday."

"You have really good taste in choosing your wardrobe."

There's nothing quite as disarming to an insulting, critical, negative person as a genuine compliment!

Then, walk away. Don't wait for the person to sputter anything else at you.

If a person puts you down in public about your business, ask a simple question, "What are you doing so you can be financially free in the next five to seven years?"

Refuse to Internalize the Negative

In many cases, we don't have to fight against any person or any company or any thing. We simply need to be excellent at what we do—excellent in our products, excellent in the service we give, excellent in our work habits, excellent in explaining our business plan or our products. Virtually any obstacle in your path can be overcome by excellence in service or personal integrity.

I have met numerous people in my life who seem constantly at war with the people in their business environment. They internalize tremendous stress because of what others around them are saying or doing.

My approach is to ignore those who are criticizing, ridiculing, degrading, or otherwise speaking or acting in a negative manner toward me. The fact is, there are always going to be some people who don't think you can make it. I chalk up their opinion as ignorance—in most cases, they don't know what they don't know.

There are also going to be a few people who don't want you to make it. I use their opinions as fuel. Their attitude motivates me to think, "I'll show YOU!" And then to work doubly hard to prove to them that not only can I make it but I am making it and will continue to make it!

I encourage you:

- ❖ Spend your efforts seeking to outperform your critics
- ❖ Work harder than your competitor is working
- ❖ Exceed the quality that is displayed by your adversary
- ❖ Achieve more than your critic achieves
- ❖ Accomplish more than your enemy accomplished

If you set yourself to out-thinking your detractor, and then out-working and out-performing him, you will have spent your energy wisely and you will leave your critics in the dust.

On the other hand, if you allow the negative things said about you or done toward you to keep you mentally occupied and emotionally drained, you will have very little output, be distracted to the point of producing very little quality, and have relatively little to show for your efforts. In the end, those who say and do negative things toward you will have succeeded—not because they were necessarily better, but because they succeeded in convincing you that you were lesser in some way.

Some people conclude part way to achieving their goal that they aren't worthy of the success they dream of achieving. Some conclude they don't have what it takes. Some conclude that success takes more effort and energy than they have to give. Their thinking results in their producing less, with less quality and less effectiveness. If you are struggling with ideas such as these, ask yourself, "Who told me that I wasn't worthy of success? Who told me that I couldn't succeed? Who told me that I don't have what it takes to be excellent or to give top-quality service?" And then ask yourself, "Why did I believe them?"

The vast majority of critical comments are not rooted in fact or substance. They are rooted in envy, a competitive spirit, or outright meanness.

Don't take any idea into your mind and harbor it unless it is positive and motivates you toward greater excellence.

Box Up the Insults and Trash Them!

If you get a big ol' load of personal insults from somebody, I advise you to box them up and then trash them.

What are personal insults? They are insults based on who you are and what you can become, not on any one thing you have done or are doing. Consider some of these comments...

- ❖ "You never were as smart as... [your brother, your sister, your cousin]..."
- ❖ "You always were a... [dummy, slow, lazy]..."
- ❖ "You're just like your mother... [or father or dead-beat uncle or off-the-wall aunt]..."
- ❖ "You can't do anything right..."
- ❖ "No one in our family has ever been..."
- ❖ "We just aren't business people in our family..."
- ❖ "You never were very good at..."

❖ "I never knew anyone who made a go of a business like this..."

If have struggled with a lot of personal criticism in your life, or you are currently receiving a lot of personal criticism, I suggest you keep an empty box in your office and each time you receive a personal insult, write it down in bold letters on a piece of paper, crumple up that piece of paper, and throw it in the box. When the box gets filled, tape it all up and take it out to the trash. Have a little ceremony as you toss out the garbage!

This Is the Nitty-Gritty: Have No Self Pity.

Chapter 11
Keep Your Eyes on Your Goal

Without a doubt, one of the most important events in my life was the adoption of my daughter Debi, and five years later, my son Paul. I didn't know anything about the birth parents of my daughter Debi at the time I adopted her. I began to look for the natural talents and abilities she might have—those aptitudes that were built in to her genetically.

As soon as Debi began to learn how to talk, I began to work with her to teach her how to sing. By the time she was three years old, she had learned "The Lord's Prayer." She sang with a sweet cherubic voice that was very endearing.

I said to her one day, "Debi, wouldn't it be fun to sing a solo in church?"

She said, "Oh no, mommy, I could never do that."

Debi was very shy. I also worked with her on skills to help her communicate with others. I'd say, "Debi, pretend that I'm Mr. So-and-So. Say hello to me." We'd role-play all week so she'd have the courage to speak to various people that we saw at church every Sunday. I knew that singing a song in front of a crowd of people would be a major feat for her.

One day I asked her, "Debi, what would you like to have more than anything?" She replied, "I would really like a backpack."

I said, "How about this? Next Sunday, I'll ask the pastor to have all the people bow their heads and close their eyes. Then you can sing 'The Lord's Prayer' while they are praying. After the church service, we'll go to the store and I'll get you the best backpack we can find."

"Really, mommy?" She was very excited.

The next Sunday, I was sitting at the organ and Debi had moved out onto the stage a little ways. The pastor had everybody bow his or her heads for prayer. All was going according to plan. I began to play and Debi began to sing, "Our Father..." And after only two measures of the song, nearly every head had come up and every eye had opened to see where this beautiful little voice was coming from!

Debi looked at me—her eyes wide with fear—and I whispered to her from the organ bench, "Backpack." She turned back toward the audience and continued, "...which art in heaven."

From me on the bench, "Backpack."

"Hallowed be Thy name."

"Backpack."

We made it through the entire song this way—phrase by phrase—neither one of us missing the beat.

Debi made it all the way through that song because the goal that was before her was greater than the fear she felt in the moment. Her vision of a backpack was stronger than her anxiety.

After the church service, we went to a store that sold backpacks and I bought Debi a fabulous backpack that was nearly as tall as she was. She was elated.

Debi learned a very important lesson of life on that day. She gained tremendous inner strength and courage. From that time on, we began to go to retirement homes and convalescent hospitals and Debi would sing as I accompanied her. By the time she was nine years old, she was singing at fairly large gatherings.

Having a goal not only helped Debi through one bout of fear related to singing in public on one occasion. Having a goal and working her way through her fear went a long way to curing her forever of that particular fear.

That's what having a positive goal can do for you! If you truly keep your eyes on the goal, you'll be able to deal with your fear. And as you conquer that fear by working through it, you'll eventually find that you are no longer afraid.

Are you afraid of making a cold call? Are you afraid of making a presentation? Are you afraid of an upcoming appointment?

Keep your eyes on the goal you have set before you!

Continue to pursue your goal regardless of how you "feel" in the moment.

Soon you won't be afraid—in fact, you likely will look forward to the next call, the next presentation, the next appointment. You'll see them as signposts that you are one step closer to your ultimate goal of success.

The Opposite of Fear is Faith That a Great Good Can Come Out of any Difficult or Negative Experience.

PART IV

Positive Motivation

Chapter 12
Discover the Stability of a Sturdy, Three-Legged Stool

For a number of years when I was a child, my father had a dairy. I know well the three-legged stool that was used by the person who milked a cow. Those three-legged stools were sturdy—they didn't tip over or collapse.

The sturdy life that doesn't collapse in a crisis or in a time of discouragement is also marked by three facets. I encourage you to cultivate them in your life.

1. Never Stop Learning

Don't limit your learning to your school years, which may include college. Don't think that all learning is associated with structured courses or training programs. Instruction is packaged in many different ways in our world today. Your goal is to find something you want to know, or to isolate something you need to know, and then find the most enjoyable and high-quality means for gaining the best instruction possible!

❖ Read books
❖ Attend guest lectures
❖ Take a short course of ten to twenty hours of instruction
❖ Go on a learning retreat or a learning vacation
❖ Keep your mind active and engaged every day of your life into finding out what's going on in the world
❖ Various functions, meetings, and weekend seminars will also be available to you in your network marketing business. Take advantage of these events!

Why? Because you'll benefit tremendously from the practical advice you receive, not only from the platform speakers but from your fellow colleagues over midnight coffee at the local café. You'll also receive encouragement from others who are in the same business you are in. The motivational speakers brought in to events are often just that—motivational. And, you'll benefit perhaps most of all from the friendships you make.

When a person tells me he is discouraged, the first two questions I ask that person are these:

❖ What have you read today?
❖ What have you listened to today?

Any person who only reads the daily paper or listens to the daily news—or listens only to music and talk shows on the radio or reads only trashy novels or gossip magazines—is going to be a person who can't help but get discouraged! Life is far more than crime and weather reports.

Have you ever stopped to think about the fact that the vast majority of the news we hear is negative? You may not be able to do a thing about an earthquake in Central America, a tornado in Texas, a cyclone in Japan, or a hurricane in Florida, but in some very small way, that negative news filters down into your mind and heart so that the world as a whole seems a little less secure, a little less welcoming, a little less safe. You may live miles away from the place where the reported murder or rape took place, but that news seeps into your mind and heart so that the world as a whole seems a little more frightening, a little more anxiety-ridden, a little more tenuous.

Shut off the negative and turn on the positive. Balance out your thinking. Listen to and read and watch videotapes of stories and experiences and accomplishments and ideas that are uplifting and challenging and encouraging!

When you stop reading and listening to positive information and ideas, you can't help but slide into negativity and discouragement. You may not be aware of this downward slide, but trust me, others around you will be aware of the change in you. They may not know why you suddenly seem more pessimistic, more downcast, or disheartened...they may not even be able to define what they sense about you that is different...but they will feel that you are more negative. In turn, they will respond to you by either ignoring you or turning away from you—after all, who wants to be around a negative person? Being rejected is only going to make you feel more discouraged!

Those who don't turn away from you may try their best to cheer you up. If they can't jolt you out of your negative doldrums, they are likely to become a little angry—their anger may very well take the form of nagging or result in an argument or take on the guise of an "I've told you before" conversation. I don't know about you, but I don't enjoy those kinds of encounters—they can leave me feeling even more discouraged!

Don't fall into the downward spiral of negativity. Keep reading and listening to those things that build you up, encourage you, inspire you, and teach you practical and positive things that will lead to your success. Keep feeding your mind and heart huge doses of what is positive.

2. Never Stop Earning

Never stop producing. From the time a child is old enough to do a few chores for money to the day a person dies, a person should be working at something. Work is effort expended for which reward is received. All genuine work, even volunteer work, has an element of reward to it.

I recently met a man who told me that he was retired and was busier than ever working. He was especially involved in building Habitat for Humanity houses and also helping older people of low income with simple home repairs. He had sufficient income. I asked him, however, if he did anything for monetary reward. He smiled a little and said, "Oh, sure. I spend an average of about ninety minutes a day managing my retirement portfolio!"

Some of this man's earning time is spent reading business-related magazines and newspapers to which he subscribes. Some of his time each day is spent checking out the stock and bond markets on the Internet. Some of his time is spent in monthly meetings with his financial advisor and investment broker.

3. Never Stop Yearning

Every person should always have dreams and goals that he or she is actively pursuing. A goal or dream that isn't being pursued is just a wish or a whim. A genuine dream or goal has a timetable and a certain amount of methodology associated with it—it has how, when, with whom, and where dimensions. For example, you can wish the purchase of a new home for decades. It's when you set a plan for saving money on a monthly basis to purchase a new home that has a specific price tag—and you start acting on that plan—that you turn your wish into a goal.

Don't stop setting goals in your life! You may have all that you need...even all that you want...but have you done all you can do to help other people achieve their dreams and goals? Have you done all that you can do to pass on what you know to the next generation? Have you done all that you can do to bless others in your family, neighborhood, community, or even a forgotten corner of the world?

Let me give you some suggestions about goal-setting:

❖ <u>Be Specific</u>. Be as concrete and specific as you can be. Becoming rich isn't a goal—it's a wish. Becoming independently wealthy isn't a goal—it's a desire or a dream that is accomplished in small steps. "I am going to earn six thousand extra dollars this coming year in my own part-time business" is a goal! That's five hundred dollars a month for twelve months.

❖ <u>Visualize What You Want</u>. I like photos and visuals that may be cut from catalogs or magazines. I feel motivated by reminders tucked into my bedroom mirror or attached with magnets to the refrigerator door. These visuals remind me why I'm working so hard. They remind me what it is that I'm hoping to have, achieve, or earn in the next few weeks, months, or perhaps even years. The photo may be one of a palm tree and a white beach—a vacation I'm hoping to have. It may be a photo of a third-world medical clinic—a venture I'm hoping to sponsor or fund. It may be a photo of a piano I'm hoping to own or a car I want to park in my garage. It may be a photo of a person in a cap and gown—the education I want to fund for my child or for a student from another nation.

Other people are motivated by writing in a journal what they hope to have...to become...to accomplish. They keep their lists of "things to do" and "things to be" and "things to own" in a place where they can read them often.

❖ Choose to Soar. Choose to be around people who are dreaming great dreams, thinking noble thoughts, and exploring the highest excellence. Great music puts musicians in touch with their inner passion to create something beautiful and noble. There's nothing more inspiring to a musician than to play through a new piece of music with other musicians who are committed to excellence. That is an experience marked by a joy few non-musicians can understand.

Truly inspiring messages—whether on tape or in print—also tap into that inner desire we all have to soar.

The vast majority of the people I have met through the years have had a deep inner desire to do something valuable or worthy in his or her life. There has been a desire to have meaningful experiences and to do something significant in this life, make a mark, and leave something good behind. That deep inner desire is kindled and rekindled in us by those who have overcoming, succeeding, winning, or make-a-difference stories. Choose to listen to them. Choose to associate with them. Choose to adopt them as your role models.

Start With Who You Are, Where You Are, and What You Know. But Don't Stop There.

Chapter 13
That Hurt Really Good!

Years ago I was with a boy named Brian as he was learning to water ski. He never gave up! When he'd fall, he'd quickly climb into the boat and say with a big grin, "Let's do that again. That hurt really good!"

It wasn't the pain that made Brian a successful young man. It was his determination that the pain was good—it was part of a learning process that he knew deep within was going to lead to his success. Sure enough, he became a good water skier. But even more importantly, he carried that same grit into everything he did so that no matter what he attempted, and no matter how much pain was involved along the way, he emerged a success.

There are sacrifices that need to be made in the start-up phase of any direct-sales business. Recognize that going in. Like all businesses, effort and investment are front-loaded. The fruit comes later! Don't expect overnight success. Don't expect immediate large returns the first few months, or even year.

My accountant once asked me, "Why would you make all the trips to this particular location and not see any return from your trips?" I smiled and said, "I'm planting good seeds and expecting a good harvest later."

That's exactly what happened. Within two years, that particular location was really producing...and I didn't need to make any more trips there for quite awhile.

When I first began my business, every promotional kit I purchased, I purchased with the sale of product. I had no money to use as a start-up fund for my business. If I wanted to attend a promotional meeting, I had to earn the money from selling products. On more than one occasion, I drove over a range of mountains to get to a promotional meeting and after the meeting—having no money for a room at a hotel—I slept in my car before driving back home the next day.

With every stage of expansion in my business, I experienced a new round of pain. The time came when I decided to move out of the comfort zone of my immediate city and state. I bought an "unlimited legs" ticket. I flew in and out of Atlanta a lot using that ticket. I took with me a little hotpot for heating water and soup, and for these appliances I took along some coffee, dried soup packets, cereal packets, and food bars. Every night, I'd make myself a little dinner in the hotel room and make my appointment calls. I got where I needed to go. I made the appointments I needed to make. I made three or four presentations a day. I didn't waste time or money eating out. And in the end, I did a lot to get my business off the ground.

Was it fun sitting in a hotel room making calls and eating hotpot food night after night? No.

Was it exciting to be spending so much time in rather boring airports and sitting on airplanes? No.

Was it exhilarating to keep this kind of schedule? No—it was exhausting.

But...it was necessary.

I learned a lot about myself during those months. I learned what I was made of. I learned my strengths—and also my limitations. I learned that it's possible to do what you have to do to succeed, but that success is never automatic. It takes work, work, and then some more work. It takes digging deep. It takes riding out the tough times and surviving the low moments. I had a little motto during that period of my life: "Cry, redo my make up, and go out again."

Whenever it was possible, I talked to the people sitting next to me on airplanes about my business. If I could tell they weren't remotely interested, I'd do my best to learn something from them that might help me in sales. If I thought there was some possibility they'd be interested...well, I just happened to have my sales materials in my carry-on bag. The first person to whom I really presented the business plan was a person I sat next to on an airplane—Rosey Grier, the former football player for the Los Angeles Rams!

Every Person Becomes Discouraged from Time to Time

I don't mind admitting to you that I became discouraged from time to time. I don't know anybody in a network marketing business that hasn't been discouraged.

I remember being particularly discouraged when I went to my first large weekend seminar. One of the women who spoke there was a very tiny Oriental woman. She couldn't even see over the lectern—they had to remove the lectern so we could see and hear her. She said in fairly broken English and in a very timid voice, "I come from Korea four year ago. Don't speak English too good. Lady come my door with some things and say, you want to buy some? Then I say, can I sell too? She say yes. I get started and work very hard. Only problem— husband die. Heart attack. Too late for me to go to school to be doctor or lawyer. I want my boys to be proud of me. So I said, I know. I work even harder selling. I learn long time ago, when you complain about problems, ninety percent people don't care. Other ten percent, glad. So I don't complain. Three years later I reach my goal. My boys proud of me. Thank you very much."

She had us all standing on our feet!

I thought to myself, "I'm twice as tall as this woman. I speak English fluently. I was born in this nation. If this woman can make it, so can I." I worked very hard and along the way, I learned what this woman had learned. If I complained about my problems or difficulties, ninety percent of the people to whom I complained didn't really care. The other ten percent, indeed, were glad! So I stopped complaining and redoubled my efforts.

Take Courage From Worthy Role Models

If you don't have a role model of courage in your life, find one! Adopt one! Develop a friendship with someone you admire who has been an overcomer. The example of that person can make a great deal of difference to you, especially in times of discouragement.

I have such a role model—my Aunt Ethel. She had a tremendous influence on my life.

During the Great Depression, Aunt Ethel lost two of her children to measles. They were seven and eight years old at the time. That was long before vaccinations had been developed against measles—we tend to forget that just a century ago, measles was a major killer of children around the world, including our own nation. Aunt Ethel was devastated at their deaths as I'm sure you can imagine. Then, to add to the misery of her life, her husband lost his job and couldn't find another one. Jobs seemed particularly scarce in rural Oklahoma where she lived.

Aunt Ethel had no particular training for a profession. She had grown up on a farm and the nearest town was just that—a town. She said to herself, "We have to have some bread in this house. What can I do?"

Even in the midst of her grief, she knew that she couldn't wallow in self-pity or sadness. Her family needed food! She quickly turned her mind and heart to the positive.

Aunt Ethel was creative. Because of their financial situation through the years, Aunt Ethel had always made her children's clothes. So, she took a few pieces of fabric that she had left over and designed some darling little dresses with full skirts and slips. She then walked door to door in the wealthy neighborhood of her town, and neighboring towns, asking the lady of each house, "Would you like to buy this little dress for your grand-daughter?"

In those days particularly, it was a good bet that the woman in residence of a substantial house was a grandmother. And then, even as we see today, it was the grandmothers who could afford to indulge in luxuries for their grandchildren...even in the Great Depression. Aunt Ethel was smart enough not to waste her time in the poorer areas of town.

Time and again, a wealthy lady would say to her, "Yes, dear, that dress is charming. I think I'd like to order another one for Suzy, another one for Mary, and another one..." Aunt Ethel would say, "When would you like to have the dresses?" Usually the time frame was just a matter of a few days. Aunt Ethel accepted their cash up front, purchased the fabric necessary, and then worked long hours into the night to finish sewing those custom-designed dresses.

In a short time, Aunt Ethel built a solid business. Even after her husband got a job, she continued to show and sell and sew. She eventually was able to move the business out of her home and set up a little factory operation. The business grew to the point that her husband left his job and became the manager of her factory!

Within ten years, she had built a million-dollar business. Her clothing line was expensive and very few stores carried her line of designer dresses for children—only the finest stores carried Aunt Ethel's creations. The stores that did carry her clothing line sold those little dresses like hotcakes and could hardly keep them in stock. The exclusivity of her designs was part of the sales strategy for her business—something she never intended but something that happened along the way.

Aunt Ethel was always beautifully dressed in silk suits when she made sales calls to these exclusive department stores or when she went to "market" in Dallas. At the factory, however, she was Aunt Ethel in work clothes. I loved to watch her work in her sweat suits and tennis shoes. She paid special attention to the buttons and zippers and lace that came from suppliers around the world.

Aunt Ethel taught me a number of things about free enterprise and selling and presenting a product line. She also taught me this: If you want to build a million-dollar business, you had better know your business and stay on top of it at all times.

I have a secretary and an office...but I know what's going on. I don't leave the operation of my business to others. I keep current with all the numbers and all the information I need to have in order to make quality decisions about how best to spend my time and energy.

It's fun for me to experience—and fun to remember and fun to tell others about—various trips abroad and resort vacations and cultural experiences I have had because I've done well in my business. But travel and concerts and plays aren't the mainstay of my life. The vast majority of my days are spent working...plain, old-fashioned, sleeves-rolled-up working. Most of my days are spent on the phone, at one-on-one appointments, in sales meetings, speaking at inspirational retreats, or pouring over lists and books and product information to stay up to the minute on what and who are turning out to be high productivity centers, and on what and who need additional encouragement or promotion.

One Christmas, my Aunt Ethel wrote me a card that said, "You and I are the kind of women that shorten the bread lines in this country. Keep it up! Love you, Aunt Ethel." That note is one of the treasures of my life.

Face Down the Temptation to Quit

I have faced a number of temptations to quit my business and "get a job." I don't know anybody who is successful in a direct-sales business that doesn't have such opportunities. Ambition, an ability to organize and motivate, and a degree of salesmanship are qualities people want to hire and attract to their own enterprises!

After I had reached one level of success in my business—a level, by the way, in which many people sustain a very nice income—I was asked to fly to Arizona to interview for a position with one of the best choral departments in the nation. The professors there were impressed with my music credentials and my reputation and they asked me to enroll in their doctoral program. They told me what I knew to be true: a degree from that program would have set me up for the best jobs in the nation as a choral instructor and adjudicator.

It was momentary temptation. But in the end, I stuck with building my business because no matter how fine a job might be in a choral department of a university...it was still a job. It wasn't my own business. The sky wasn't the limit.

Every job has associated with it a ceiling on income as well as a certain amount of internal politics, schedules imposed by others, and limitations associated with vacation time. Building my own business was far tougher—at least initially—than any job when it came to hours and effort, but in the end, building my own business has no ceiling on income, no internal politics, no schedules dictated by others, and no limitations on vacation time!

Building your own business may be harder work initially, but in the end, that work pays off in a way the work of a job never can.

Some time later, I was approached by a dear friend who has been my mentor in the music business for more than twenty-five years. He currently is the chairman of the National Association of Choral Conductors. He said, "Beverly, it's time for you to quit messing around with that business. You've done what you need to do. It's time for you to come back to us now. I want to offer you one of the finest choirs in California. Come and take it."

I said, "I appreciate the offer. Thank you very much, but I have a much greater calling."

At this point, I consider myself to be absolutely unemployable. Nobody can hold out a job for me that will be as good as the satisfaction and rewards of my own business.

Refuse To Quit

There's no need to belabor the point. As you face temptations to quit, just say "no." I had to tell myself often, "Beverly, starting isn't finishing."

You Have the Ability to Compensate for Any Difficulty.

Chapter 14
Success is the Quality of Your Journey

Success comes as you make the journey. Success is how you feel about who you are, what you are accomplishing, and what you are thinking, dreaming, and achieving. It isn't about how you feel about your past, what you have accomplished, or what you once achieved, dreamed, or thought. Success is an ever-present doing process. Success is the quality of your journey. It isn't a destination point.

James Dobson has been a friend of mine for years. He told me about his father's death and he said with a certain amount of sadness in his voice that his father had left an unfinished painting on his easel. I said, "Jim, that's exactly what life should be all about! We should be creating and producing until the day we die. We should never look back and say we 'finished' anything—we should still be in process of working at our dreams and goals."

I always want to be on my way to somewhere. I always want to be going and producing and working. That doesn't mean that I don't want to have times of relaxation and sheer fun. It does mean that I want to thoroughly enjoy every minute of my life. I want to enjoy every conversation and friendship as it happens.

Yesterday I took a couple minutes out of my day and just stared at a hummingbird outside my window. The day before, I took a five-minute vacation to a faraway place after browsing through a travel brochure. Often, I spend some time soaking in my bathtub and playing CDs for complete relaxation.

I have learned to enjoy now.

It's the success you experience along the way and as part of the journey that puts a quickness to your step, a twinkle to your eye, and a light behind your smile.

Don't postpone your life. You can hold out dreams and goals to your spouse and children but don't postpone building your relationship with that spouse or that child on the way toward the accomplishment of your goal. Find ways to build in quality time. Find ways to make the mundane moments fun. Take time to listen and to appreciate what your spouse or children are saying to you.

Gentleman, you might hold out the promise of a new car to your wife, but in truth, what she'd really like is five minutes of your time today. She'd like for you to look her in the eyes and say, "Honey, is there anything I can do for you? I appreciate so much all that you do for me."

Lady, you may hold out the dream of a new bicycle to your eight-your-old son, but in truth, what your son would really like is for you to listen to how he hit the ball into left field and made it all the way to third base today.

Take Joy in the Moment

I have a friend whose son contracted AIDS. She shared with me a little of the frustration she had felt with people assuming her son was homosexual, when in truth, he contracted the disease from a blood transfusion. She shared a little of the fear she had for his future and her own as his mother. But mostly she shared with me the tremendous change that had come into her life as a result of her son's diagnosis.

She said, "Beverly, we live every day with a great surge of hope. We pay attention to the little things of life. We enjoy the small moments, the little bits of beauty, the sunrise and the sunset, the flowers that are suddenly in bloom by the walk. We take time to really listen to each other. We make an intentional effort to express how much we love each other and to say 'thank you,' 'I appreciate you,' and 'I value you' in as many ways as we can."

She then added with a sigh, "It's the way we all should live every day of our lives...but it seems to take something like AIDS, doesn't it, to force us to live the way we should live?"

Enjoy the Work

Most of the time I don't call what I do in my business work. I see what I do as being fun and challenging.

Only you can decide how you will feel about your work and how you will approach your work.

If you approach various tasks as drudgery, you will soon feel exhausted.

If you see your work as a burden, you will collapse under the weight of it.

If you can hardly wait until you get to the next level so you won't have to work as hard, prepare to be disappointed. There are challenges at every level of any business.

Reaching a goal is exciting and exhilarating. Reaching a new high in any endeavor can result in an emotional high. What we need to recognize is that it's not enough in life to feel fulfilled only after we reach a goal. The journey toward a goal can be just as exciting, just as rewarding, just as fulfilling if we choose to enjoy the tasks we are doing, enjoy the people we are meeting, and enjoy the process of building a business.

Take joy in helping new people achieve their dreams.

Take joy in seeing others in your organization move ahead and overcome their obstacles.

Celebrate their successes. In truth, their successes are propelling you toward a new level of success in your life.

Make the Troublesome or Burdensome Person Your Special "Project."

We all have troublesome people in our lives. Sometimes they are people we live with...sometimes people we work with... sometimes people who just happen to cross our path in any given day.

I have had a simple approach to troublesome or burdensome people: I make them a project. I suggest you do this for those in your network or those who are prospective recruits who turn out to be people who seem to be more trouble than they are worth.

Don't have an attitude of "I sure wish he'd quit so I wouldn't have to answer so many of his questions." Don't have an attitude of "produce or get out." Instead, see a person who bugs you as being a potential asset in your future and as a work in progress. That person needs your training, patience, encouragement, and expertise. If there's a particular type of person that seems always to annoy you, address that annoyance in yourself—the fact is, you are going to encounter that type of person again and again. You can choose either to live your life in a perpetual state of annoyance and frustration, or learn to accommodate that person in a positive way and help them be less troublesome.

Smother your enemies with kindness. Find out what a troublesome person likes and then give some of that to the person. Express genuine concern. Give a genuine compliment. Win that person to your side!

In many cases, a person is troublesome or annoying because he is poorly informed or poorly trained, has a great need for your attention, feels threatened by you or is jealous of you, or is undergoing a difficult time in his own personal life. Get to the root cause, as best you can, of why a person does what he does and then seek to address that root cause, not just the symptomatic behaviors.

Be Thankful

Choose to have an attitude of gratitude.

Be thankful for what you have and what you are able to do.

Be thankful for the blessings you have received in life.

Be thankful that you are intelligent.

Be thankful that you have a house to live in and a car to drive and sufficient food and clothing.

Be thankful for your good health, and if you aren't in good health, be thankful for the medical care available to you so you might improve your health.

Be thankful that you live in the nation in which you live.

Be thankful that you have friends and acquaintances that are there for you if you have a need.

Be thankful for your children, and if you don't have children, be thankful for those children that you are privileged to love and influence.

Be thankful for your business. Be thankful that you have an opportunity to become more prosperous tomorrow than you are today.

Smile Anyway

Always serve your clients or associates with a smile, regardless how you feel or the circumstances of your life. Any time you answer the phone, answer it with a smile in your voice. Send the message that you enjoy what you are doing and that you especially enjoy the opportunity to see or to help your client or associate.

Sometimes you need to smile through your own mistakes and foibles!

I was five years old when I experienced my first Christmas play. It was a major event in my life. My mother helped my sister and me rehearse our lines. I was to hold a tinsel star and recite a two-line rhyme. When it came my turn to speak, I boldly blurted out my sister's lines! I had heard them so often I just automatically recited them, and quickly added, "Oh shoot, that was Barbara's part." Of course the audience cracked up and didn't hear my lines, and my sister was very angry that I had already delivered her part!

Throughout my life I've had a number of opportunities to laugh my way through mistakes far bigger than delivering my sister's line in a Christmas play.

I was in an airport recently and I had my ID in my hand, ready to show it. I tossed my latte cup into the trashcan and the minute that cup left my hand, I thought, "Something wasn't quite right about that." Sure enough, I had tossed my driver's license into the trash.

I took a look at that fairly large trashcan and burst out laughing. I thought, "This is going to be a sight. Here I am in my St. John knit ensemble, rings on my fingers, and a thousand-dollar carry-on bag slung over my shoulder, and I'm about to go headfirst into this trashcan to dig out one small piece of laminated paper!" Ridiculous looking or not, that's exactly what I did.

I took off the lid of that trashcan and dove into it like a homeless person looking for part of a leftover sandwich. A driver's license doesn't just lay on top of the trash, of course. It has a way of sliding down the sides into who knows where. But I kept searching until I found it because the simple fact was...I had to. I wasn't going anywhere without that license which was my ID to get on the plane. I didn't care what people thought. I had a goal!

Sometimes you simply need to choose to see the funny side of life's situations.

Generally speaking, when I'm not a hundred percent sure where an appointment or meeting is, I leave the house a little early and then, if I find the location with a few minutes to spare, I drive on to the next block, set my timer, and take a quick five-minute power nap. I'm grateful I can do that because a five-minute nap can really energize me.

One evening as I did this, I saw a woman run out of her house and across the street. A few seconds later, a man ran out of the same house after her. I thought, "Wow, I'm about to see a fight." That isn't at all what happened! As I watched these two people crouch behind a hedge, a Cadillac pulled up in front of their house. Two very well dressed people got out, one with a briefcase. They went to the door and rang the bell. They looked at each other, rang the bell again, and looked at their watches. They glanced toward the windows of the house and finally they walked back to their car and drove away.

I hadn't watched a family fight. I had watched a no show!

I felt like rolling down the window of my car and calling to them, "Hey, they're behind the fence over here!" I didn't. But I did enjoy a good laugh.

There are always funny things that happen to you in the direct-sales business. Savor those funny things as being funny.

Take Time to Regroup

Know your limits—physically and emotionally. There are times when you need to get away and rejuvenate. It may be an hour that you lock yourself into your bathroom for a soaking bath and some personal pampering. It may be an evening out with a friend. It may be a weekend away that's just for fun. Nobody can work 24-7 and stay healthy.

For the most part, I encounter people who need to be motivated to take action, not to take rest, but from time to time I do encounter people who are all work and no play. Being a workaholic is not healthy, any more than being any other kind of "holic" is. Those who work to the point of failing to eat and sleep sufficiently, or who work to the point where they forget how to laugh, are people who are heading for serious health problems or job burn-out. An excellent book on health and nutrition for busy professionals is *The Healthy Executive* by Amy Sutton (SuccessDNA 2002). Just thirty minutes a day can make all the difference. Above all, take time to exercise...to play with your children...to attend a concert or play. Have a massage...get a pedicure...walk along the beach or stroll through a beautiful garden or park...pause to take in a beautiful sunset.

I frequently take a five-minute vacation by closing my eyes and imagining myself in a far-away exotic location. I take off my shoes, put my feet up, sip a cold drink through a straw, and dream away! Sometimes I take an afternoon off just to sit by the pool or go to a day spa.

I once asked a very successful friend of mine what she does to unwind. This friend is also in a direct-sales business and her answer was a little unorthodox, but I found it to be great advice! She said, "I put on my jeans and sweatshirt and sunhat and go out and get in my Rolls Royce. I drive down the road to the river, park my car, and get out and go down to the river with my fishing pole and fish for awhile. It doesn't matter if I catch anything or not. I pull my hat down and fish all day long."

Fishing may not be your thing, but there's something that is relaxing and enjoyable to you that's legal and moral. Take time to do that fun thing in your life.

Now I ask you...

Is the person who knows how and when to relax and have fun...who knows how to deal with troublesome people...who has the ability to laugh and enjoy life's simple pleasures and his own foibles...and who has developed a true pleasure in his work a successful person? In my book...YES!

People Get No Satisfaction out of Laughing at a Relaxed, Joyful and Positive Person Who is Laughing, Too!

Chapter 15
Write Your Own Book

I recommend that every person I know keep a journal...and keep that journal with him at all times. Keep the same size journal and date each one as you make your first entry. Then, every time you go to a meeting, an inspirational retreat, or have an appointment with your supervisor or mentor, write notes to yourself in your journal. There are several benefits to this.

First, having your journal and a pen poised to write also makes you much more intentional and eager to receive what others say to you. If you have your journal open and your pen ready to write, you likely will find that you are looking for nuggets of truth, practical advice, or innovative suggestions in a much more intentional way than if you are just sitting back with your arms folded. Having a journal says to both you and the speaker, "I'm ready to take in all that you have to give me." It puts you in readiness mode.

I'll never forget the first time I got off a plane in India at midnight and was greeted by about thirty of my business associates, each of them with a journal and pen ready to take down everything I had to say that might help them grow their business. They were ready and eager to listen...and as a result, I was even more ready to share all I could!

Second, you'll find that when you write a journal, you shift from being a passive participant to being an active participant in the communication process.

You may never have thought about this, but the fact is, far more people have a better visual memory than auditory memory. In other words, they remember what they see more readily than they remember what they hear. When you write what you hear in a journal, you shift from being auditory-only to being both auditory and visual. The end result is that you learn more—you are quicker to apply what you learn and quicker to remember it.

Third, you have a back-up for your memory. In case your memory fails you, you have a record of what was said. It's down in black and white for your review in times when you are feeling discouraged, puzzled, or have doubts about yourself and your ability to succeed. It's there for your perusal any time you have a few minutes to muse about the direction your life is going.

So many times in a one-on-one counseling appointment, a person will sit across from me, listen, and nod, but not write down anything. I'm quick to say, "I know you think you're taking in all that I'm saying, but trust me, you aren't. Write down some of what I'm telling you. That's the only way you truly are going to remember it later."

Fourth, you have a source of ongoing inspiration and education. Sometimes people will say things you aren't quite ready to hear in the moment—you don't have enough background information or life experience to fully understand their message. Sometimes you may be a little preoccupied with a problem or feel stressed out. Reading back through a journal can be a valuable means of learning or re-learning key concepts at a time when you are able to understand them, apply them, and benefit from them.

"But I have a tape recorder," people say.

It's not the same. In the first place, people look back through journals far more quickly than they re-listen to tapes. In the second place, people do not invest anything of themselves in the recording of a tape. They do invest something of themselves in the process of writing in a journal. There's far greater ownership for a written journal than for an audio tape of an appointment or interview. There's greater value placed upon the ideas that have been expressed in the journal.

What Should You Write?

In addition to the pearls of wisdom you receive from others...in addition to names and dates and places that you may need to recall or follow up on later...use your journal to record:

- ❖ A Record of Your Successes. Your journal is a good place to record your successes and how you feel about them. Take note of every milestone. Have you just made your first solo presentation or made your first sale? Take note of that! Have you reached a new sales record? Have you reached a new income level? Have you reached a particular award status? Acknowledge and celebrate your own successes! Give yourself a written pat on the back.

- ❖ A Record of Your Feelings. As you conduct your business, periodically note in your journal how you are feeling about your business in general. Many of your feelings are likely to be ones of discouragement or weariness. That's one of the reasons its important to note your successes so that you'll have a reference point to balance off those times when you feel like throwing in the towel.

If you note that you are discouraged, try to identify why you are discouraged. Is it because you haven't been reading or listening to enough positive input? Is it because you lack training? Is it because you feel you are failing in a particular aspect of your business?

Then, next to each discouragement, write down what you believe to be the remedy for that discouragement. Your prescription for your own improvement may be to listen to more tapes, reprioritize your schedule, find a way to streamline an aspect of your business, get additional training, or any number of other practical remedies.

Focus on the answer to your problem or need...and get busy acting on that answer. Your discouragement is likely to dissipate very soon.

The Book You Write is Ultimately the Best One For You To Read!

Chapter 16
It Has to be You

The main lyric of a popular love song a number of years ago said simply, "It had to be you."

Well, when it comes to staying positively motivated, the ball is in your court. Ultimately, it's up to you to motivate yourself. Other people can share their stories and words of inspiration...but you have to choose to be inspired by what they say. Other people can call to encourage you...but you have to choose to receive their encouragement and internalize it.

Through the years I've spoken to a number of conferences in a program slot that was titled "Attitude Session."

Most of us need to have our attitudes adjusted from time to time.

What Do You Think of YOU?

It doesn't make any difference if you're driving a beat-up ol' car with the front seat ripped and a tuna sandwich from last week under the back seat.

It doesn't matter if your furniture is from Salvation Army and your appliances were all purchased at garage sales.

It doesn't matter what other people say about you or to you as you start your business.

What matters—and hear me well, the only thing that really matters—is what you think of yourself on the inside.

Even when I was at the bottom of the heap, I felt on the inside that I was a winner and that I was going to find a way to get to the top of the heap. I didn't know how...I didn't know when it would happen...but I believed that it both could happen and would happen.

I saw myself as a successful, generous, giving person who had an ability to motivate other people, help other people, and do something worthwhile in this world.

The fact is...

It doesn't matter if you have a chauffer who drives you around in a Rolls Royce and you dine in the finest restaurants.

It doesn't matter if your furniture is all imported from the finest antique dealers in Europe and your appliances blend into your kitchen so well your guests can't figure out which door to open to find the milk.

What matters—yes, the only thing that really matters—is who you know yourself to be on the inside.

Who do you see yourself as being, and as becoming?

In the network marketing business, we often focus our attention on what we need to do. Who we need to call...what we need to order...what we need to say...what we need to learn...what we need to teach...where we need to go and what we need to do to get there.

It's just as important to spend some time periodically reflecting on what you want to be as a person. What character quality do you want to develop? What attribute do you want others to recognize and appreciate in you?

It's important to develop a definition of the kind of role model you want to be to others. What is it that you seek to impart to the next generation...to the new recruit...to the person less fortunate than you...to the person from another nation that you encounter on his or her home soil?

Fill your mind with positive pictures about who you WANT to be.

Whom do you want to be like?

Whom do you want to serve?

What do you want to accomplish?

What do you want to do for your community?

Stay Young At Heart

Choose to think young no matter what the calendar or the mirror may say!

You think you're still young...if you think your birthday should be a national holiday.

You think you're still young...if you still cry at sad movies and laugh at happy ones.

You think you're still young...if you think chocolate is one of the major food groups.

You think you're still young...if you enjoy licking the batter from the spatula.

You think you're still young...if you still enjoy going barefoot.

You think you're still young...if you always save room for dessert.

You think you're still young...if you still believe in your dreams and are fearless in the face of a new challenge.

I encourage you to take some time to study the children around you. Children know how to dream. They aren't afraid to tell you what they dream of being...how they want to live...and what they want to accomplish when they grow up.

Children are willing to try...and try again. None of us would have ever learned to walk if we had given up the first ten times we fell to the floor after taking a step or two!

Children are eager to learn. In fact, some people who have studied children believe that learning is the greatest high most children experience from day to day. They love exploring new ways of doing things, meeting new people who can tell them interesting things about life, trying their hand at new skills, and taking on a new challenge, whether it's a great tree to climb or a new computer game.

Children truly believe they can do anything. They believe they can fly...they just haven't learned how to get airborne yet! They believe they can conquer the world. They believe they can do just about anything they set their minds and hearts to do. And who says we can't fly? Are we all that far away from individual airborne transport systems? And who says we can't conquer the world—at least impact the world and conquer certain aspects of its poverty, illiteracy, and disease rates? And who says we can't do just about anything we truly set our minds and heart to do? Rather than encourage children to get realistic about life, we probably need to become more daring and enthusiastic and creative as adults!

Children know how to have a good time along the way. They don't wait to have fun later. They choose to have fun doing just about everything they do from hour to hour! When my daughter Debi was a little girl, she loved to have tea parties. And I loved to have them with her! It took very little time and effort to put out cookies and hot chocolate and sit down and pretend to be ladies at tea. Have fun with the people you work alongside and the people you speak to, meet with, and attempt to recruit!

There's no reason not to dream...not to learn something new...not to take on a challenge...not to believe in things that are not yet a reality...not to have a good time in your life. There's every reason to have these childlike attributes!

Move Toward Your Future

A sure-fire way to have an automobile accident is to drive looking at your rear-view mirror instead of at the road that lies ahead. The same is true in life.

There are times when you simply need to draw the shade on the past and move toward your future. There comes a point when you need to stop blaming your mother or father or teacher or coach or former spouse for what they did or didn't do for you...and start doing positive things for yourself.

It's not the aunt who told you that you weren't pretty enough...

It's not the teacher who told you that you weren't as smart as your older brother...

It's not the coach who told you that you weren't good enough to make the team...

It's not the step-parent who told you that you were worthless and that you'd never amount of anything...

It's not anyone in the past that is responsible for your future failure or low self-esteem. You are responsible for who you are today and what you decide to make of yourself, which will determine who you are tomorrow.

The truth is, only you can improve your self-esteem. Nobody else is responsible for how you feel about yourself...and frankly, nobody else can make you feel better about yourself until you decide that you are a worthy, valuable person.

Choose to like yourself the way you are, and to believe for the way you still want to grow, develop, and become better. I read a saying just recently that gave me a smile: "Like yourself now. Be ten years ahead of your friends!"

It's one hundred percent acceptable to like yourself. It's a far better alternative than not liking yourself!

That doesn't mean there aren't things about yourself that you don't want to change. A desire for positive change is at the root of all good growth and development. But...appreciate who you are as a person. Appreciate the talents and abilities that have been built into you. Appreciate the personality that you have been given. Appreciate your own sense of humor, your own intelligence, your own curiosity, ambition, dreams, idiosyncrasies, foibles, and the myriad of experience that you have had in your life.

A healthy self-esteem is very important to people in any business. Part of selling is selling oneself...and selling oneself generally involves a healthy dose of self-confidence.

If you need to do something to feel better about yourself, then I encourage you to get busy and do it. For example, if you need to lose weight, get involved in a weight-loss and exercise program and especially involve yourself in a program that has a group component to it. You'll be more committed to the program and stick with it longer. Meet some other fun, disciplined people—you may very well end up recruiting some of them to your business.

I encourage you to read books that help you build your self-esteem and become more self-motivated.

Some people seem to think that pride and a very positive self-esteem are one and the same. They aren't. A highly positive self-esteem says, "I'm valuable. I'm worthy. I'm as good as the next person when it comes to receiving God's love and having something positive to contribute to this world." Pride, on the other hand, says, "I'm more valuable and more worthy than other people."

Self-esteem says, "I have a special set of talents and abilities, and therefore, I have something to give to this world." Pride, in contrast, says, "The world ought to give something to me because I'm special."

No Room for Pride

There's no place for pride in a network marketing company—if you think other people owe you a living, you will soon find yourself sorely discouraged. However, there's every place for positive self-esteem in network marketing. A positive self-esteem is the engine that drives the motivational car—it's the force that says, "Hey, self, let's get in gear and see what all we can accomplish here. Let's give this everything we've got because what we've got is good and what we are likely to earn and receive back from our effort is also good...very good."

Choose to be a person who is in the process of becoming the person you ultimately want to be! An old sign hung over the counter at a general store in Texas: I ain't what I ought ta be. I ain't what I'm gonna be. But I ain't what I was.

No Room for Revenge

Part of having a healthy self-esteem is leaving behind attitudes that are rooted in revenge. "Just you wait Henry Higgins" may have been a good motivation to Eliza in *My Fair Lady*. I know many people who start out in their businesses motivated by an attitude of "Watch me succeed! I'll show you!" aimed at a former boyfriend or spouse, a dismissive coach, or a person who was part of the clique or group that rejected their participation. You may be able to fuel your motivation for a while on hatred or feelings of vengeance, but in the long haul, maintaining that posture is going to reinforce your negative self-attitude and self-worth. Subconsciously, you will continue to say to yourself, "They said I'm not worthy and I'm going to prove that I am." Why remind yourself at all about what others have said or thought?

A healthy self-esteem says, "I know how valuable I am and I'm going to express my value by setting high goals and achieving them!" A healthy self-esteem says, "I don't care what others think of me—not really, not ultimately. I only care what God says about me and He says I'm loved, forgiven, and eternally valuable to Him. I choose to think about myself what God thinks about me." A healthy self-esteem says, "I know who I am and I know where I'm going. Come run with me!"

Only You Can Talk Yourself Out Of Laziness

One of the most successful women I've ever met in a direct-sales business doesn't drive an automobile. I can't imagine how I would live if I couldn't drive. She is handicapped and does what she can.

This woman takes the bus to her meetings and delivers products to her customers by taking a bus! She did this for years, and built a major business. I'm so glad much of her work can now be done using computerized ordering and direct delivery.

I don't accept any excuses about traffic or about how difficult it is to get to a customer. I just tell them about Barbara.

When somebody tells me that he or she can't drive forty miles to a meeting because it has rained and the freeways might be a little slick...

When somebody tells me that they consider it "hard work" to make five phone calls just to get one appointment...

When people complain that they have to stay at home alone with the children in the evening because their husband is out making a presentation...

My response is, "Get serious!"

I know a friend who has an associate that is truly inspiring. This man once was a prisoner of war in Vietnam, confined to a bamboo cage. He didn't know if he was going to live from one hour to the next, and if he was allowed to live, whether he would be given anything to eat on any given day.

He said to my friend, "Dave, I just can't relate to those people in this organization who tell me that they have a fear of using the phone."

I know a couple that left the Soviet Union because they had a dream of a better life for themselves and their family. They rarely talk about any struggles they have now or have had in the past. They consider all their struggles simply experiences they had on their way to getting where they are now and where they still dream of going. I once asked them how they felt about making cold calls. They said, in somewhat broken English, "It's no big deal! We do whatever we have to do. We did hard labor in Russia!"

I know a couple that came from Africa because they wanted to have a business of their own. They have overcome all kinds of obstacles with language and unfamiliarity with American customs and fear of making presentations. They literally faked it until they made it. They never gave up. They never thought it was too difficult to make ten phone calls and three presentations a week.

Only You Can Decide to Live a Positive Life and Be a Positive Person

The plain and simple fact is that people respond more to people who are positive than to people who are negative. People as a whole want to be around people who are encouraging, uplifting, hopeful, energetic, optimistic, enthusiastic about life, and filled with joy. People as a whole seek to avoid those who are critical, cynical, sarcastic, pessimistic, bored with life, depressed, or in despair. You can choose the attitude you have. Even in situations that are negative, you can choose to have a positive response.

In some area of your life, there's a significant likelihood that you need to have an attitude adjustment. Every person I've ever met goes through bouts of self-doubt, negativity, and discouragement about something, or perhaps someone. We continually need to recognize areas where we need to adjust our attitude toward the positive setting of the dial...and then make the adjustment.

Only you can do it!

The Starting Point for Change is With Yourself.

Chapter 17
Did You Hear What You Just Said?

"I just can't remember names."

"Nothing ever goes right for me."

"I just can't seem to get organized."

"This is going to be one of those days—I can just feel it."

"I already know I'm not going to like it."

"I never have enough time."

"I'm just no good."

"I can't seem to get anything done."

"I'm just not cut out for that."

"If only I had more time...."

"If only I had more money....

Have you ever said or thought any of the above statements?

Negative self-talk is always rooted in "I can't" and "I don't have" and "I'm not" statements. These are statements of failure even before any attempt has been made!

Rather than speak the negative, begin telling yourself what you need to do and then, what you will do or will be once your attitude has been adjusted.

Begin to speak positive, motivating statements to yourself, such as:

"I can sell."

"I need to get in gear."

"I ought to make some calls."

"I should start taking this business more seriously."

"I know I can do this if I'll just make the effort."

"I need to make five calls today and try to set up at least one appointment."

These are statements that redirect your mind and attitude toward action. Just thinking these thoughts or even voicing these statements aloud isn't action, but they do refocus your attention toward positive behavior.

Change the Way You Talk to Yourself

"Dear me, I look terrible. Why did I stay up so late? Just look at those bags under your eyes. I've got such a headache. I've gotta get to work and I sure don't feel like it. I don't have money for parking because I forgot to cash that check. This is going to be a miserable day."

"I'm going to make it through this day just fine! I just need to jump in a hot shower, take my high-potency vitamins, and get going. I can borrow money from somebody for parking until I get that check cashed later today. It's going to be a great day!"

Which of those two sets of statements above is going to result in your having a better attitude, more energy, and greater motivation an hour after you think or speak them?

Do you ever have conversations with yourself? Do you sometimes feel as if you are at war with your inner self? Who wins that war?

If you are going to have a conversation with yourself, have a conversation that is aimed at moving your mind from the negative end of the thought spectrum to the positive end!

Speak as if You've Already Arrived

Speak to yourself as if you've already made the attitude adjustment. Here are some sample statements:

"I no longer have a fear of making a phone call to invite a person to an informational meeting."

"I no longer have a problem with my self-esteem."

"I no longer care what others say about my business."

"I no longer allow my feelings to be hurt if somebody says 'no' to the products or business opportunity I present to them."

"But," you may be saying to yourself, "you're just fooling yourself."

Yes, perhaps...but not for long. The more you tell yourself that you aren't going to be intimidated by another person, the less intimidated you feel and the less intimidated you act

---

when you are in their presence! The more you rehearse mentally how you are going to feel when you make a phone call, the less anxiety you will feel about making that call...and the less anxious you will actually be once you have the phone in your hand. You are literally speaking into reality the attitudes and opinions that you want to instill in your mind. You are speaking to your mind what will be the new attitudinal habit.

When I was teaching my children to brush their teeth, I made them brush their teeth every night before they went to bed. I reminded them nightly to brush their teeth. I watched them brush their teeth. I built a habit into their life. After a while, going to bed just didn't feel right to them until after their teeth were brushed.

To a very great extent the thoughts of our minds are habitual. We either get on a negative cycle and build a negative attitudinal habit...or we put ourselves on a positive cycle and build positive attitudinal habits. To move from the negative to the positive, we have to purposely make ourselves think certain thoughts and voice certain thoughts. We are literally building new mental pathways along which our thoughts can run. Once a new mental pathway or attitudinal habit is in place, a person doesn't have to continually say to himself or herself, "I'm not fearful" or "I no longer have a problem with..." The fact is, that person just isn't fearful and no longer has the problem! Attitude has been adjusted!

There's a general process involved here for most people. It's a matter of moving from "I can't" to "I ought to" to "I'm going to" to "I'm doing it!"

I can't tell you what causes a person to move from one step to the next. Sometimes people are just so fed up with what their life has been like, is now, or seems it always will be that they shift into high gear and never look back. At other times, people seem to inch forward toward a change in their life. They spend a long time convincing themselves that they can do something different and ought to do something different.

Your role as a motivator is to recognize the level of resistance a person has and to help them move to the next step. Give the person both reasons and encouragement to believe they can succeed...they ought to give the business a try...they can do what it takes...they need to act now (and often).

Here are some examples of positive affirmations:

"I enjoy being responsible."

"I'm in charge of me and that's a challenge I enjoy."

"I am trustworthy."

"I meet my deadlines."

"I can be counted on."

"I am a success."

"I never worry."

"I choose to look at the world around me in the bright healthy light of optimism.

"I always and automatically think in a decisive and determined way."

"I have accepted responsibility for myself."

Come up with your own set of positive affirmations. Write them down in your journal. Read them often...and read them aloud. Write them out on 3 x 5-inch cards and tuck them into the visor of your car or into the edge of the bathroom mirror.

Why Say This Aloud to Yourself?

Because what you say is internalized by you and it becomes part of your thinking and believing, and in turn, part of your speaking and behaving.

Why speak aloud? Because what your own two ears hear you say is even more effective than what you hear another person say. You are the foremost person influenced by what you say.

When should you engage in self-talk? I suggest that you engage in self-talk while you are driving on your way to a sales presentation or to an appointment with a prospective recruit.

"But isn't this just giving myself a pep talk?"

Yes! That's exactly what it is. But if you don't give yourself a pep talk, who will? Pep talks work.

What You Say to Yourself Determines Your Energy Level

Have you ever had a down day in which you felt totally depleted of energy and enthusiasm...and then suddenly, you received some good news—perhaps a check showed up in the mail that was greater than what you had anticipated. Almost immediately, you felt more energy and enthusiasm. In reality, nothing had changed physically. You hadn't had a nap or a massage or been out for a good brisk cardiovascular walk. The only difference had been a shot of good news. Well...if good news doesn't come from the outside, generate it! Speak good news to yourself, or if you can't seem to muster up enough energy for that, pop an inspirational tape into the car stereo or a tape recorder at home and listen to a dose of positive, motivating news and opinion from somebody else.

As I neared major goals in my business, I sometimes found myself "sleeping on excitement." I had a deep enthusiasm and energy that had nothing to do with how much sleep I was getting, how nutritionally I was eating, or how much exercise I was getting. I was on a success-in-the-making high! Trust me...that's a GOOD feeling!

Say Something to Yourself That's Worth Hearing.

Chapter 18
Keep Pedaling!

Many years ago I was invited by a group of teachers to go out on a motorcycle weekend with them. I had been given a motorcycle about two weeks before this time. We must have looked like a modern caravan. About seventy-five teachers participated—some came with pick-ups and tents, some with campers or motor homes. We had been riding the goat trails in the desert for a couple of days and I was pretty much over my fascination with my new motorcycle. I was also pretty tired from the weekend of peer pressure and from riding over bumpy trails. I was riding in about a foot of sand at the end of the trail—very glad to be heading for home. I made the mistake of cutting the gas and turning the bike at the same time. The bike, of course, sank in the sand and stopped cold. I went flying. I broke my leg in seven places.

I had no idea that this one moment would change my life so dramatically. It took eight hours for my friends to get me to the hospital. The physicians there told me I'd never walk again.

Nine months later, after many prayers, many treatments, and countless hours in rehab, I walked.

Through the course of my life since then, however, I was not able to walk normally, even with four surgeries. Finally I had knee replacement surgery. When the physician came to talk to me after the operation, he said, "I've never seen a knee that bad. You've been living in tremendous pain for a lot of years, haven't you?" That sounded like the understatement of the century to me.

I hope people didn't notice that I limped a little, or that a grimace of pain crossed my face from time to time. I never wanted my leg or my pain to be an issue for anybody...including myself! It took a lot for me to finally say, "If I am going to improve the overall quality of my life, I need to stop doing all that I'm doing and have this surgery."

My friends had been encouraging me to have the surgery for years. So had various physicians. It was only when I finally decided for myself that I was going to have the surgery that I actually had the surgery. Nobody else could make that decision for me.

I had to cancel five trips that I really wanted to take. I had to set aside my normal schedule and adopt a new schedule. I had to discipline myself in ways I hadn't disciplined myself in years.

The same was true for me at the time I started my marketing business. People had been encouraging me for years to make changes. I didn't listen. It was only when my old life became unbearable and the hope of a new life with less financial pain became the dream of my heart that I was willing to take the plunge. It required of me the same thing a knee replacement surgery required—setting aside my old ways of spending my time and energy and adopting some new disciplines.

I knew the surgery would be painful but I had no idea how difficult the months of rehabilitation would be. I heard people say, "Oh, my grandmother had that surgery and she's doing just fine." They never told me how long it took before she was doing fine! Let me tell you, when I awoke in recovery, I wanted to die from the pain. My children and my love for them flashed through my mind. I knew my business was doing fine. It seemed like a good time to go on to heaven!

Friends encouraged me when I was released from recovery to a private hospital room. They said, "Beverly, you are going to make it! You will make it!" That isn't what I wanted to hear.

This happened to me, too, as I started my business. The first few weeks were very tough. I had a major learning curve to conquer. I felt like quitting on more than one occasion. But friends kept telling me, "You can do this!"

A machine was hooked up to my leg and its purpose was to move my leg whether I wanted to move it or not. That machine moved my leg for twenty-four hours without stopping. As the hours passed, the tension and angle of the machine were changed. After a day or so, the machine was only hooked up at night. Have you ever tried to sleep with a machine slowly moving your leg all night long? There finally came the day when the therapists told me that I could no longer rely on that machine—I had to lift and move my leg on my own strength. As much as I tried, I couldn't seem to will some of my muscles that hadn't been used for more than twenty-five years into the precise action I wanted them to take. It took tremendous effort. But I did it. I knew I had to if I was going to walk again without any type of cane or support. I had lots of ups and downs in therapy. Therapy overall was a humbling experience for me—I often didn't want to do what my very agile and youthful therapists wanted me to do.

The same was true in the early months of my business. The day came when my sponsor said, "I'm not going with you on appointments anymore. I'm not going to make presentations on your behalf anymore. You're on your own. You can do it." It took tremendous effort. But I did it. I knew I had to if I was going to build a business that would lead to financial independence.

In many ways, the starting of a new business was humbling. I was a musician...I was a college instructor...I was a professional!

I've encountered a number of people through the years who have felt humbled at starting over in a career—they may have been doctors, dentists, lawyers, or people with a long career in another profession. Developing a network marketing business is something new—it's starting over from ground zero.

Starting over is what I had to do when I relearned how to walk with my new knee. Muscles needed to be retrained and strengthened. It was a long process. My therapists often used language I didn't understand. I had to trust they knew what they were talking about and that they knew something about making my leg stronger that I didn't know.

Again, that's what happens in the first stages of developing a network marketing business. I had to learn new jargon. So does every person who starts a new endeavor. I had to trust that the training I was receiving from my organization would help me grow a successful business.

For weeks after my knee surgery, I lived by three exercise prescriptions given to me by my physical therapists: "Do this thirty times, three times a day...Do this ten times, three times a day...Bend this far, straighten you leg, lift it up, walk backwards, walk normally." I didn't like living by these prescriptions for my recovery. But I did live by them.

I also lived by the prescription to give myself a shot in the stomach every night for weeks after I left the hospital. This was to keep my blood from clotting and sending dangerous clots to my heart and brain. Did I enjoy doing this? Of course not! But the realization of what could happen if I didn't give myself those shots was motivating!

In sharp contrast to the prescriptions, which meant pain, I received banks of flowers...and visits from encouraging friends, including four young girls who came to sing to me, "We love you just like you are"...and e-mails from people who thanked me for various things I had done to help them. I was overwhelmed by these expressions of genuine affection.

I felt as if I was living between two extremes—the pain of the therapy and the joy of the encouragement.

My first months in the business, I also lived between two extremes. I was being told by my sponsor, "Do this. Do that. Give out this. Make this many calls. Host this many meetings." It was painful at times, but it was the prescription for my success. I knew that I didn't want the alternative. I had lived on the edge of the alternative and I didn't want to live in that state for the rest of my life!

Along with the directives related to various network marketing skills and techniques, I received a great deal of encouragement, "You can do it. You can make it. I'm here to help you. I believe in you."

After a couple of months, I didn't have to give myself the shots anymore, or to exercise quite as hard—at least the exercise didn't seem quite as hard. That was true in my business as well. There came a time when I suddenly realized, "I know a little bit about what I'm doing here! I'm starting to receive rewards and I like them!"

One of the things my therapists told me to do was to ride an exercise bicycle every day. Actually, at the time, that seemed a lot less painful than some of the things I had been doing! I belonged to a nice health club and I went regularly to swim and then sit in the hot tub afterward. No problem, I thought.

I quickly discovered that going back to that health club after knee surgery was not at all like going there before knee surgery.

For one thing, I couldn't climb the steps in front. I had to use a handicapped-vehicle sticker to park in back and go through the handicapped entrance. I couldn't get in the pool and hot tub. I was to ride a bicycle for fifteen minutes. They may as well have told me I had to climb Mount Everest. Fifteen minutes on an exercise bike seemed like forever. Just getting on that bicycle took tremendous effort.

I thought, "I used to do this so easily...now I can't do it at all!" It took me quite awhile to figure out how to use my cane and some other support devices to get myself up on the bicycle seat and my feet into the stirrup holders on the pedals. Just as I discovered that my muscles had forgotten how to walk, I discovered that my legs didn't remember how to pedal a bicycle!

As I was struggling to get situated on that bicycle, wearing old shorts and no make-up, the television set above me came on. A video by Mariah Carey came on and the lyric she sang washed over my soul like soothing balm, "When you feel that hope is gone, you look inside you and be strong, and you'll find that it is true, that a hero lies in you."

I started crying from the pain of getting my feet into the pedal stirrups and the tender hope of this singer's message. I began to move those pedals slowly, but surely, saying under my breath, "You're not going to defeat me, bicycle. I'm going to do this. I'm going to go around and around until there's no more pain." And I pedaled and pedaled. For weeks, I pedaled and pedaled. And I pushed through that pain and my knee got stronger and stronger.

And today...I walk the way I did before the motorcycle accident.

Are you crying from the pain today that it's hard to be in business, hard to make ten more calls, hard to give one more presentation, hard to drive the miles, hard to hear criticism or rejection?

Keep pedaling.

Work through that pain.

You can make it. You will get stronger if you keep pedaling. And you'll not only survive, but you'll discover that there is a hero inside you.

The Road to Success is Uphill All the Way.

Chapter 19
Anticipate the Turn-Around Moment

I got my driver's license when I was fourteen. That was possible in Texas because I lived on a dairy farm with my parents and farm kids were allowed to drive in order to help with farm chores.

Well, I didn't do a lot of driving for the dairy, but I did drive.

One day shortly after I got my license, my father told me that he was selling the dairy because the price of milk had dropped dramatically and we could no longer make a decent living by running a dairy. He then told me that we were going to move. He said, "I'm driving the truck and you'll need to drive the family car because your mother is too sick to make the trip." So, we moved to Victoria, four hundred miles south, leaving my mother behind temporarily.

I followed my dad's tail-lights the entire way, with no money in my purse, my little white dog beside me, and my knuckles white on the steering wheel in sheer terror because in spite of having a license to drive, I didn't really know how to drive!

We got there after dark, unloaded a couple of mattresses, and made up two beds. The next morning, Dad made coffee. He looked at me and said, "Do you want to try coffee?"

I wanted to be tough and strong like my dad so I said, "Sure." He said, "You can't drink anything in it. You have to drink it black." I agreed. It tasted horrible to me but I drank my cup because Dad drank his cup.

Then Dad said, "I've hired two men. You set up the house while I'm out. I've got to find a job." And he left.

I told the men where to put all the furniture in that three-bedroom house, unpacked the dishes and other boxes of items and put them away, and then set out to enroll myself in school.

I grew up quick!

Since that time, my Dad and I have had a special bond and part of that bond has been sharing coffee together—strong, black coffee. When I'd go to visit him, he often brought me a cup of coffee first thing in the morning. We'd sit down and talk over the day ahead.

A few years ago, I took my parents to Hawaii. My father was in such bad shape with his weak knees that the two of us made a pact: "We're both going to have the knee surgeries we need and we're going to walk on the beach together when we get well."

One week after my knee surgery, my eighty-three-year-old father had his surgery. He had some complications—the surgeons were never really certain but they thought he might have suffered a stroke during the operation—and Dad couldn't swallow. Besides getting over the pain of the therapy, Dad had to cope with a feeding tube down his throat.

I started to feel stupid for complaining about my therapy with my Dad coping with even more discomfort. I thought to myself, "At least you can eat, Beverly!" For ten days, Dad couldn't eat. Finally, they allowed him to eat some mashed potatoes.

Then came the day when my sister was visiting Dad in the hospital and the nurse brought her a cup of coffee. Dad looked at her and said, "You give me a drink of that coffee!" She did.

She told me, "Dad took that cup with both of his hands, put it to his lips and took a drink. Then he held that coffee in his mouth for a while before he swallowed it. He relished the taste."

I knew in that moment that Dad was going to be OK. It was the major turn-around moment in his recovery.

Anticipate the Day You KNOW You will Succeed

Do you remember the Hans Christian Andersen fairytale about the ugly duckling? The other ducks made fun of him to the point that he wandered over to another pond. He started swimming with the swans there and one day he looked down and saw his reflection in the water—he wasn't ugly or a duckling...he was a beautiful swan!

Maybe this is you. On your job you feel out of place, as if you are in the wrong pond. When you start your own business and associate with other entrepreneurs, you will see just who you are—a beautiful swan!

Anticipate the day when you realize that you really DO know what you are doing.

Anticipate the day when you realize that you ARE making GOOD money in your business.

Anticipate the day when you know you WILL succeed.

Anticipate the day when you realize that you have reached financial independence and security.

How others see your potential is not at all accurate in the vast majority of cases. Most people don't think you can...don't believe you will...can't imagine that you are...question whether you should...and won't believe it when you do. The sad fact is that most people will look at your life and judge you by the same scale that they are judging their own life. They will see you through the lens of their own failure, their own limitations, and their own average dreams and achievements.

Don't picture your life according to someone else's opinions of your potential for success! Don't paint dreams of your future according to their expectations! Set your own dreams, have your own expectations, and develop your own opinions about your success.

The old saying is still true: Whether you believe you can or can't...you're right. If you believe you can...and you work hard to prove yourself right...you will succeed in reaching the goals you are pursuing. If you believe you can't...well, you probably won't work much at all...and you'll fail just as you thought you would.

Anticipate the Day When a "No" Turns Into a "Yes"

So often, people who are involved in a network marketing business become discouraged because they take "no" answers as personal rejection. The fact is, a "no" today from someone may not be a "no" tomorrow.

I broke up with a boyfriend the night before I left for college. It was something I knew I had to do to start a new life. We were up pretty late that night saying a rather emotional good-bye. The next day, in driving from Texas toward California with my mother, I fell asleep during the afternoon...while I was driving. The car rolled three times and ended up off the road in what seemed like the middle of a desert.

I came to my senses and realized I was alright, but my mother was unconscious and moaning nearby—I felt sure I had killed her. Our luggage was scattered all over the place, as were some of my clothes. The car was demolished.

I thought, "This is a great way to start my new life as a college student. I kill my mother, break up with my boyfriend, destroy my car, and am feeling totally worthless and scattered."

Finally, police arrived and then an ambulance. Mother was taken to the hospital where she was diagnosed with a sprained back, but was otherwise alright. I told the police my father worked for Immigration so immigration officers arrived not long after. In the end, two immigration officers drove me the rest of the eight hundred miles I had to travel to get to college.

I arrived in California to face a battery of tests that were part of the orientation process at the college. The results from one of the tests caused some alarm in the folks who administered the test. It was a psychological test! Their becoming alarmed meant that I became alarmed! Apparently the test revealed that I was deeply disturbed, possibly even psychotic, and that I needed serious counseling and watching, and perhaps wasn't ready for college.

When they began to share some of these results with me, I told them about the trauma I had just been through in the days before I took the test. They agreed that I could retake the test, and this time, the results were far different.

Every time you go into an appointment—whether it is an interview setting, a sales call, a corporate meeting, or any other kind of business encounter—recognize that you don't know what the other person is going through in their personal life, or perhaps has just recently experienced. Whatever you do is going to be laid on the foundation of what they are feeling and thinking. Their response to what you say and do may not at all be the response they would have a week from now or a month from now.

If someone rejects your idea, scoffs at your sales pitch, or criticizes your opinion...don't take it personally. In all likelihood, to a great extent, their response to you is an extension of their response to something else that is happening in their own life.

Give a person another chance. If a person tells you "no" once, don't take that as a "no" forever. Go back to the person after a period of time and try again. This time their personal situation may be very different and they may be much more receptive to what you are saying, selling, or soliciting.

Recognize, too, that corporations change and grow. If your corporation has added new products or services in the last five years, go back to those you may have contacted in the past and say, "Hey, I know you weren't interested in the past, but I'd like to show you how things have changed since then."

Sometimes people just aren't at a place in their life where they are ready for a challenge.

I've talked to people who thought they really were going to soar in their careers. They weren't interested in what I had to say.

Ten years later when they weren't soaring as they had hoped, they were interested.

I've talked to people who had no interest whatsoever in hearing words like retirement and secure income. They had no interest in building financial independence. Fifteen years later, which was fifteen years closer to retirement, they suddenly awoke and realized they weren't going to be able to retire in the style they had hoped. They were very interested in hearing what I had to say.

I've talked to people who tried a direct-sales business with a product line that they weren't truly enthusiastic about. They got discouraged and gave up. They weren't at all interested in hearing me talk about a network marketing business. But seven years later, when they saw my success and realized the quality of the products and services offered by the corporation with which I'm associated...they were interested.

I've talked to people who were so wrapped up in their corporate job they had no interest in starting over in their own business. Nine years later when they were down-sized right out of that job, they had to start over and they decided to do it in a way that could build financial independence.

Don't be reluctant to revisit old rejections. This time, you might find acceptance, and even if you don't, your contact will be better informed about what you do for a living and about the goods and services your corporation offers. They may still say "no" but they may also refer you this time to a person who will say "yes."

The Most Important Moment in Your Life is THIS Moment and What You Do in It. It's Really the Only Moment Over Which You Have Control.

Chapter 20
Let a New Dream Propel You Forward

Early in my business, I drove a Volkswagen. I had worn a VW for many years—and I use that word "worn" intentionally. I'm tall and when I get in a VW, there isn't much room for anyone or anything else. I dreamed for years of having a different car, especially one with defrost. For those of you who have never owned a VW, defrost in a VW is a window open and a soft rag to mop up the moisture. In the Northwest, that's not a very comfortable way to drive around town.

I heard at a motivational seminar that I should find a photo of something that I dreamed of having, doing, or owning. Then, the seminar speaker advised that I put that photo in a conspicuous place where I would see it often. Well, I decided that I would find a photo of my dream car and I would put it in on my refrigerator, which truly was the most conspicuous place that I saw often!

I thought about my dream car for a while before I found a photo of it. I decided...

My dream car needed to be BIG—it would be a car that I didn't have to wear but could drive.

My dream car would need to have a backseat speaker for the radio—since in my VW I felt as if I was already sitting in the back seat.

My dream car would have knee room. My dream car didn't need to have leg room—I didn't know enough to dream about leg room. I dreamed of just having knee room.

I finally decided that my dream car was the biggest Cadillac being manufactured. I found a picture of my dream car and put it on the refrigerator. It hung there for two years. I'd say to myself frequently, "Someday I'm going to have a car like that!"

It was a dream.

Then one day a man I knew called me and said, "Beverly, I have found a really great deal on a car."

I said, "I'm not getting a new car until I can get the car that's just like the picture hanging on my refrigerator."

He said, "I don't know what kind of car you have hanging on your refrigerator but let me tell you about this deal. It's a really great car and a great deal."

I agreed to hear what he had to say and he started in, "Well, it's the biggest Cadillac being made."

I said, "What color is it?"

He said, "They call it midnight blue."

Guess what color I'd been staring at for two years? Midnight blue!

I said, "Jimmy, does it have a defrost?"

He said, "Every Cadillac has a defrost! You can dial in whatever temperature you want the car to be."

I said, "Does it have a backseat speaker?"

He said, "This car has quadraphonic sound."

I said, "Can you adjust the seats?"

He said, "You can adjust them every which way you can imagine."

He told me the deal about the price and I did some quick calculations and I decided I had made enough money that I could afford this car, and let me tell you, it was a great experience to drive home in that midnight-blue Cadillac. I had the windows rolled up, the sound system on, the seat adjusted just perfectly, and the temperature dialed down to sixty-eight degrees.

I honked at total strangers and waved. I drove into the service stations where I had taken my old VW and said to the attendants there, "Mine. All mine."

Yes, that car was a dream. And it was a great day when my first dream came true. I had worked hard to turn the dream into a reality, but the reality was certainly sweet when it arrived.

But what happened after that dream came true? Why...I started over with a new dream!

In more recent years, I dreamed about owning a nine-foot grand piano that I saw and played while I was in Vienna. Very specifically, my dream was to purchase a Bosendorfer grand, which has five extra keys on it. I dreamed about this piano and I kept a photograph of this piano on my refrigerator. There was only one problem I could foresee—this piano cost ninety thousand dollars.

I shared my dream at a meeting with some of my key associates and afterwards, a couple came to me and said, "We can't believe you named that particular brand of grand piano. We know the sales rep for that line of pianos and he has told us he can get any piano we want for half price!" Wow—in an instant, I saved forty-five thousand dollars!

When you speak your dreams, many times you will find very practical information coming back to you to help you turn your dreams into reality. That doesn't mean, of course, that I encourage you to tell every person you meet that you are dreaming of owning or doing or accomplishing a particular thing in your life. Some people will think you are out of your mind...others will think you are a snob...others will think you are asking them for something. There are select times and places, however, when it is very appropriate to tell your dreams.

Just recently, I developed a new dream and I shared it with those in attendance at a large marketing seminar in India. I walked into this particular meeting to see several hundred people staring at me as if to say, "What can this blonde American woman in a red dress possibly say to us?"

My first line to them was, "I have come to your nation to make a lot of money."

That made them squirm a little—not only was I a blonde American woman in a red dress but I was a brazen and greedy blonde American woman in a red dress. I quickly added, "And I intend to leave that money in your nation."

Now I had their attention.

I said, "I have a dream for your nation. I have friends here who are building a hospital in Calcutta—they are building it in a very poor part of the city that is in desperate need of better health care. I have a dream of building a wing onto that hospital. Will you help me do it?"

The audience stood almost immediately with clapping and cheers! Absolutely they wanted to help me build that hospital!

Was that the right time and place to share that particular dream? Most definitely! My dream became their dream and it galvanized that particular group into great and enthusiastic action.

Dreams have tremendous power to propel a person forward.

If you focus on something that is really important to you, you'll find yourself moving toward that goal in phenomenal ways—sometimes in ways that seem nearly miraculous. The more powerful your dream or goal, the more powerful its drawing power. The stronger the drawing power, the harder you seem to work and the more things seem to fall into place, and the sooner you seem to reach your goal. I don't understand how this works, but I know that it does. It has worked in my life and in the lives of dozens upon dozens of people I know and with whom I have worked through the years.

The story is told about a man who went fishing. He carried with him a ten-inch ruler. Any fish that was bigger than ten inches were fish that he quickly threw back into the water.

Now most people value big fish more than little fish. In fact, the bigger the better! Bigger fish mean fewer fish to make a meal.

A man who observed what this fisherman was doing asked him, "Why are you measuring each fish and throwing back the big ones?"

He said dryly, "My frying pan is only ten inches across."

There are some people who need to buy a bigger frying pan!

There are people who need a bigger dream.

Hold on to your small dream until you reach it. But then, expand your dream.

Don't Settle for Mediocrity—You have Potentiality!

PART V

Positive Links

Chapter 21
In Sum, Learn to Sell

Shortly after I began my business, I went to a woman who was very high on the organizational chart of my corporation. I told her, "I'm in your down-line." Actually, thousands of people were in her down-line at that time. I said, "Now that you are at the top, what do you do with your time?" She answered me very bluntly but politely, "Why, I sell and sponsor...what do you do?"

Sell and sponsor is the phrase that sums up all network marketing activity.

Every person is a potential buyer.

Every person is a potential user of your products.

Every person is a potential recruit to your business.

Every person has a network of acquaintances, friends, family members, colleagues, and people they routinely encounter as they shop and keep their lives in general repair.

One day not long ago I pulled into a gas station I have frequented for several years. I was driving a new car! The attendant came out and said, "How on earth were you able to purchase a car like this?"

"I purchased it from the earnings of my business." I then told him the business I was in and asked him, "Have you ever used any of the products?"

"Yeah," he said, and he named one particular item that he used to use. I responded, "What size do you want, when do you want it—today or tomorrow, and where do you want it delivered?"

He grinned. After he placed an order I asked him if I could meet with him to show him how he could get that product wholesale. We made an appointment.

So, Who Should You Sponsor?

I once received a greeting card that said, in essence: In the race of life, there are long-distance runners, middle-distance runners, and sprinters...and there are also some people who sit on the sidelines and make jokes about how some of the runners look in their shorts.

How true that is!

A man once introduced a friend as a person who is "highly evaluative." He didn't want to use the word "critical" but that's what he meant. He said, "My friend evaluates everything on a scale of like to dislike." Many of us do that, generally speaking toward the dislike end of the scale. Two people rarely discuss the sterling character qualities of a third person—that just doesn't make for juicy gossip.

What does this have to do with your business?

Through the years I've noted that many people evaluate potential recruits solely on the basis of their appearance, including the style of clothes they wear, the kind of vehicle they drive, and the jewelry that drips from their wrists and fingers. These people are often stunned to discover that a person whom they consider to be uglier and less stylish than they are rises to a level above their own in a direct-sales business. "Can you believe she made it to that level?" "Who would have ever thought they would rise to that position—just look at the way they dress and the funny way they talk!"

A good marketing business isn't built on looks, reputation, or matters of style. It's based on passing out information, making appointments, making presentations, selling product, and recruiting folks who are willing to do the same. That's it.

I've seen people of all races, ages, and cultural backgrounds make it in direct sales. I've seen unattractive, unstylish, unsophisticated people make it. I've seen both men and women make it to the top. I've seen happily married, sadly married, happily single, and yes, even sadly single people make it.

But...I've never seen a lazy, self-preoccupied person make it.

Here's the profile of the person I look for as a recruit to my business:

Characteristic 1: Service

I must admit that I am a big tipper. I enjoy rewarding people who give me good service. I especially enjoy people who take special care of me without any idea that they are going to be tipped (or that they are going to be tipped extravagantly).

My family and I were in New York City one time and we took a carriage drive through Central Park. Our driver went out of his way to point out various things to us and to answer our questions. He truly made us feel special and he obviously enjoyed talking about a city he loved. We tipped him fifty dollars. He was stunned. And we were happy to make his day—he certainly had made ours.

There is no substitute for good service or for having a "how can I help you more" attitude. Generally speaking, people who demonstrate good service are people who:

❖ Enjoy their work
❖ Take pleasure in helping other people
❖ Are on the lookout for ways to make another person's experience or life more enjoyable
❖ Find personal satisfaction in expressing kindness

That's the kind of person I want to work alongside!

Characteristic 2: Busy or broke or both

One of the main reasons I hear from people who resist the idea of becoming involved in a direct-sales business is this: "I'm just too busy right now to consider this."

My response is, "Of course you are!"

Busy...ambitious...successful...eager...self-motivated people are always too busy to take on one more project or responsibility. It's also true, however, that if you want a project to succeed, you should find one of the busiest people you know to head it up. Busy, ambitious, successful, eager, self-motivated people tend to be very good project managers and very good personal time managers.

We each make time for what we want to do.

If you are looking for somebody to recruit to your business, look for somebody who is very busy in quality activities. That person knows how to manage time and get things done. Your challenge will be to show that person that they need to adjust a couple of things they are doing so they can reap greater rewards in their life. It's far easier to direct part of a busy person's life toward a direct-sales business than it is to motivate a do-nothing person into developing ambition and self-motivation.

I recently heard about a couple that had been recruited in a small town in Oregon. I could relate. They receive six hundred dollars a month from Social Security. That's their sole income. They have just started a business and they are saving to buy basic information materials. Very few people start a direct-sales business as low as they are financially...but some do. And many times, it's the person who is in the hole who is desperate enough...hungry enough...motivated enough...to do the work and make the sacrifices that are necessary to really build a business. People who are at the bottom aren't in direct sales as a hobby. They don't play at business. They WORK!

A fox was chasing a little rabbit in the field. Two men were watching the chase and they were amazed at how fast the rabbit scampered in its attempts to outrun the much larger fox.

One of the men commented, "Look at that rabbit! It dodges one way and then the next..."

The other man said, "Yeah. But consider what's at stake. The fox is running for his dinner. The rabbit is running for its life."

I felt as if I was running for my life for three years as I built my business.

I don't take many excuses from people who aren't running. Running is the only speed I know for achieving success.

Running the race to success is a lot like running a marathon. There are a lot of people to cheer you on at the beginning—"Hey, go for it! You can do it! You'll make it!" There are people at the goal line saying, "Terrific, you did it!"

In between the crowds are gone and the miles stretch on and the motivation to keep going is entirely up to you.

<u>Characteristic 3: Ambition</u>

I recently took a day off to meet some of my college girlfriends in Carmel, California. I spent the night there and walked the beach and had a great time.

While I was in line at the San Jose airport for my return flight home, I met a man who is in a business similar to mine. He does business in China, as I do, and we began to talk about the various restrictions and obstacles that we had encountered there as part of the manufacturing and distributing processes. I asked him if he had ever heard of Robert Kiyosaki's book, *Rich Dad, Poor Dad*. He hadn't, but as soon as he made that admission, a young man about twenty years old standing near us piped up and said, "I've read that book. That's a really good book."

I asked him who had given him the book and he replied, "My mother-in-law." I was amazed that he had a mother-in-law...he looked too young to be married. In conversing further with this young man, I learned that he was married and that he made his living by selling Kirby vacuum cleaners door to door. I said, "Write your name on the back of my card. I'm going to call you when I get home and tell you about a business opportunity. If you're as ambitious as I think you are, you, you could gain financial freedom for you and your family within a few years of hard work."

At this point, the gentleman who did business in China looked at me as if to say, "Way to go. Wish I would have thought to recruit him."

Always keep your eyes open for people who exhibit ambition.

<u>Characteristic 4: Young</u>

For many years, people who were seeking to recruit others to direct-sales businesses tended to look to older people who had become a little disillusioned with corporate America or their first (or second or third) jobs. Others looked for people who were discouraged at their inability to pay their bills, afford a college education for their children, or who were disappointed in the growth of their retirement funds. All of those people still make good prospects, but don't overlook the young people who are just out of high school or just out of college. Their peers and colleagues are an untapped market— not only for your product, but as recruits to the business.

Two up-and-coming associates of mine have only been in the business two years and they are on a rapid rise. They were nineteen and twenty-one years old when they began their business. They were newly married—she was a hairdresser and he was a blue-collar worker. They didn't have any business experience. What they did have was a lot of ambition, big dreams, and the benefit of an older couple that could mentor them in the more practical aspects of running a business.

Young people are eager to pursue the lifestyle of their dreams. Many of them have grown up with luxuries that they don't want to give up now that they are out on their own or newly married. Others don't have any desire, or need, to go to college and they are eager to do something "on their own"—to have a business of their own and to begin to build that business into a successful career. Look for young people who have:

- ❖ Great ambition
- ❖ A willingness to put in long hours and work hard
- ❖ Are teachable, and willing to learn how to run their own business
- ❖ Reliable, especially in following through on what they say they are going to do

Characteristic 5: People You Believe Can Make It

It is vitally important that you recruit people into your business that you can believe in, and it is tough to believe in a person unless you respect that person. Choose to recruit people with integrity, honesty, and high moral values. Beyond that, you need to sponsor people whom you truly believe can succeed in a marketing business.

There are certain qualities I look for in a recruit—a willingness to work hard, a hunger for something more, a basic ability to relate to other people and a desire to communicate with others, and an eagerness to learn and try something new. No, I don't sponsor people I don't believe can make it...but I have sponsored people who weren't at all sure about themselves. Self-doubt is a natural part of starting any new endeavor.

A significant portion of my time is spent in one-on-one counseling and mentoring with new recruits. And the heart of my message to them is this: "I believe in you. You can do this."

At some point, every recruit becomes discouraged. A major factor in many people overcoming discouragement is this: Somebody believed in them and they didn't want to disappoint that person who believed in them.

Eventually, the "I believe in you" spirit transfers to the recruit. He or she or they as a couple start believing in themselves!

That's belief transfer!

The final stage of belief transfer is when the person in whom you placed your belief recruits someone under him and then pours himself into that person and believes in him until he can believe in himself! When the belief cycle moves on from one to the next to the next then belief transfer is fully in effect.

Your goal as a coach is to build leadership into other people. Part of your training needs to be training in how to mentor others, how to encourage others, how to lead, how to inspire and build up and express belief.

See Every Person and Every Encounter as an Opportunity

I'm always a little amused when people tell me, "I've run out of names of people to call to present my product or to present a sales plan." I feel like asking, "Did you stop living?"

New people are always coming across your path. You encounter them as you travel, as you talk to people while you are doing your errands, and as you go to the beauty shop or the barber shop.

When Ray Kroc first walked into the first McDonald's hamburger stand, he didn't just see the hamburgers lined up on the grill and the milkshake machines whirring away. He saw an opportunity. That's the key word to keep in mind as you encounter every new person in your life. Here's an opportunity.

Now don't be too quick to add words after "opportunity." Every person is an opportunity for you, but not every person is an opportunity for you to make a sale. Every person does represent an opportunity for service on your part. There's some way that you can help that person!

Certainly if you truly respect the company for which you are working and highly regard the quality and value of the products you are selling, your opportunity for service is going to include offering a person the chance to benefit from your products.

But don't limit your concept of service to your products. Your service to another person may be to lend a listening ear...to give that person some practical information or advice that you've learned over the years...to do something nice for that person...or perhaps even pray for that person.

Sell...sponsor...or serve. Every person you meet today holds out the opportunity for a sale, a sponsorship, or an opportunity for you to give service.

Keep Your Eyes and Ears Open, But Most of All, Keep Your Heart Open.

Chapter 22
Become a Student of People

Many people who are in network marketing think they are in the business of selling product. It is so much more. Network marketing is about people. I spend the majority of my time now recruiting new people to the business, motivating people to continue in the business, and training people in how to achieve maximum success in the business.

To become good with people, you need to study people. Consider the following four classifications of people as you recruit. They tend to be motivated by different things. Know that in advance!

Class 1: DINK—Double Income, No Kids

These are great people for you to sponsor and recruit to your business. The people who fall into this category tend to have dreams and ambitions. They tend to want things they don't presently have. They generally are willing to work hard to achieve their goals. They are often motivated by the idea that they can achieve financial independence and enjoy a very nice lifestyle within the next five to seven years if they will throw all of their energies into building a business and making temporary sacrifices now for tremendous rewards later.

Class 2: DICE—Double Income, Children, and Everything Else

These people are working hard and are generally pulled into a thousand directions at the same time. They see the bills piling up as their children grow older—and especially so as their children reach the teen years and college costs begin to loom on the horizon. They are often motivated by the need for extra income to get them through a decade or so of high expenses.

Class 3: OINK—One Income, No Kids

This category is for single people who only have themselves to support. Their motivations are the most diverse of the four groups. Some are motivated by the idea of financial independence. Some are young women who are motivated by the idea that they'd like to get married in a few years and at that time, quit work and raise children. They find the idea of an ongoing income very appealing. Still others are motivated by the idea of creating a business that will fund their retirement plans. Some of the motivation may be an opportunity to work alongside other people who are positive and ambitious and have like values related to work and success.

Class 4: SPICE—Single, With Children, and Everything Else

This is the category of single parents. Their world tends to be marked by bills, bills, and more bills. They feel the full burden of supporting themselves and their children, even if they receive regular child support. They are generally motivated by the idea that they can reap immediate rewards from a part-time effort that is run from the home—and later, reap very good rewards from a home-based business.

Adapt to Others—Don't Ask Them to Adapt to You

Always attempt to accommodate and adapt to the person with whom you are communicating. Don't expect them to get on your wave length—get on theirs!

If I'm dealing with a business person, I use business language. If a sharply dressed business person sits down next to me on an airplane, I'm likely to ask what line of work he or she is in, and if the person is in a regular retail or sales position, I might say, "Have you ever taken a look at interactive marketing or distribution technology trends?" After some discussion I might point out that a lot of people are bypassing the retail stores these days. There is now a way to take advantage of that trend and get a percentage of the sales created.

I have friends who are proof that opposites really do attract. They were married many years, happily so, even though they were very different in their personalities. The husband, who died just recently, was an extremely orderly, punctual, and precise person in all he did. When they would invite me to breakfast, the husband would tell me that he was serving breakfast at approximately 8:22. I'm prone to being a little late so I usually arrived at 8:25. His wife, however, always had just one more phone call to make and she arrived in the breakfast room at 8:40.

I loved watching these two live out their relationship and I also enjoyed watching how they interacted with other people. The husband loved detail, detail, detail. The wife loved and continues to love laughter and fun experiences.

Personality makes a tremendous difference in how you interact with a potential client or customer.

If I'm meeting with a choleric personality type, I go straight to the bottom line: "You can make a lot of money in this business and achieve financial security for the rest of your life. Are you interested?" Obviously I don't open with that line, but everything I say is geared toward the financial rewards that can be reaped.

If I'm dealing with a life-is-in-the-process person, I usually invite the person to a couple of fun events and we chat about the business around the edges of whatever else we are doing. I don't bore the person with the details. Along the way, it's the process person who usually needs to be encouraged to hire an assistant to keep track of orders and reports. This personality type also needs to be encouraged to learn how to close the deal with a potential customer or recruit. The amiable person never wants to offend and never wants to be rejected...there are times when it is better to get a "no" and move on than to waste time and energy.

If I'm dealing with an extremely analytical person, I go into all the facts and figures I can. This personality type can hardly ever get enough details. I frequently refer them to tapes or brochures that can answer their questions rather than take the time to give all the answers myself, but then I encourage the person with a smile, "You can get a tremendous amount of information and still not build a business. Unless you actually get motivated to make calls and tell people about what you do, you won't go anywhere." The problem with an analytical person is that they can easily become paralyzed.

Learn how to work with people of many different personality types.

One of the first things I do when I go to Asian countries is to sit down! I'm over six feet tall and if I don't sit down, I'm scary to Asian people.

If I'm talking to a couple in their home, I don't power dress in my most expensive suits and jewelry. I use my conversational voice, not my presentation voice. I gear the opening conversation to the décor of the room, the family photos on display, and the women's magazines on the coffee table.

Do your best to relate to the person on their level and in the context of their life.

Seek Out the Hidden Goldmine in the People Around You

I was a music teacher in an inner-city high school in the Los Angeles area during the late 1960s. Those were difficult years in L.A. The city had experienced massive and highly destructive riots—every race seemed prejudiced against every other race. It was a time of sit-downs, shut-downs, and heavy drug use in the city as a whole. My job was to try to help the kids have some legal FUN at school. I was responsible for the school assemblies, the music program, and for working with the cheerleaders and song and flag girls.

One day I was in the choral room after school. I was absolutely exhausted. The janitor, a black man who was in his late sixties at the time, had become a friend over the months. He walked into the choral room that afternoon and said, "Beverly, how's it going?"

I said, "Tom, it's really tough."

He said, "I know, I know. It's tough sometimes to know what to do."

Tom continued on with his work, pushing his broom and humming to himself. I said to him, "That song you're humming—isn't that 'Chestnuts roasting on an open fire'?"

He smiled and said, "Yes."

I said, "Sing it for me." I went over to the piano, found a key that was comfortable for him, and he began to sing. The man had a voice like Nat King Cole. I was astounded. I said, "Tom, nobody told me you could sing!"

He said, "Aw, I just sing to myself while I'm pushing my broom. I really enjoy it."

I said, "You're the star of our Christmas program this year—you just didn't know it! This is going to be your coming out party."

I wrote a background choral piece for the choir. I told them, "I've got a superstar coming in to sing this solo and if you work really hard and learn these parts, I think I can convince him to perform with us at the Christmas program if he can work it into his schedule. He'll be here in a couple of weeks and I'll see if I can talk him into practicing with us."

Well, the kids worked hard! They were in the mood for a superstar to sing with them. They definitely were envisioning someone from Hollywood. I'd hear the kids saying to one another, "We'd better be really good."

In the afternoons after school I'd practice with Tom. He was excited as a kid. During the day, he'd come by the choral room and stand outside and listen to the kids do their oohs and aahs and other back-up parts.

The day of the concert arrived. Because we had no auditorium at that school, we could only do concerts in "shifts"—students would come in during their English-class period to fill the choral room. The choral students pretty much had the day off from regular classes—in all, we sang six one-hour concerts that day.

Tom wore his black turtleneck and pants under his overalls. He came into the room with his broom and stood in the back of the room. Then, when the music started and the students began to do their introduction, he took off his overalls, moved to center stage, and began to belt out, "Chestnuts roasting on an open fire!" The students went wild. They began to whistle and shout, "All right, Tom!" They had no idea that someone in their midst had such a fantastic voice.

By the fifth concert, students were skipping class so they could come back and hear Tom again.

You should have seen Tom's face that day. He felt extremely honored. Many years later I ran into Tom. He was in a restaurant with his entire family. One of his children said to me, "You don't know what that did for my Dad. He talks about that experience all the time."

Everybody needs an occasional moment in the sun—a time when they are appreciated and recognized as being a person of talent.

There are countless people around you who have never been told that they are someone special. They've never had anyone believe in them or tell them that they can become something great. They need your encouragement to believe that they can use their hidden talents and abilities, and succeed in life.

Develop a Desire to Help Others Develop. Don't Wait Until You are Successful to Help Others—Start Now.

Chapter 23
Would You Like a Cookie?

A direct-sales business, in my opinion, is a lot like making chocolate chip cookies.

Now I don't do a lot of baking but believe me, when I do make chocolate chip cookies, they're good. Along the way, I taste the dough. After I bake the cookies, I have to taste a couple of them just to make sure they are as good as the dough told me they'd be. Then after they are cool, I arrange them on a nice platter. When my friends come over for an evening in my home, I offer them a cookie.

One friend might say, "No, thank you, perhaps a little later."

Another friend might say, "Yes. I'll take two. I'm starving."

Another might say, "Yes, I'll take one, thank you."

Another might say, "No. I don't like chocolate chip cookies, and besides that, I'm dieting."

Now, did the cookies change because of the way my friends responded? No! The cookies stayed just as excellent as they were when I took them out of the oven.

Just as the response of others doesn't change the nature of the cookies you bake, neither does it change the quality of the products or services you are offering to a person. Neither does it change the excellence of the opportunity you may be offering to a person to be part of your business.

Take confidence in the outstanding and unchanging nature of your products, services, and business. If you aren't involved in a company that produces quality products or engages in business in a quality, ethical, or legal manner—be concerned! The wisest thing you can do is find the BEST products, services, and business structure you know and devote your efforts to building a business within that organization.

People may respond to you with a

No...

Later...

Maybe...

Or YES!

Take what they say and walk away with your head held high, your shoulders squared, a smile on your face, and an eagerness in your heart to offer your particular cookies to the next person you encounter!

Once I came to recognize fully that my job was to offer good cookies...and that a person's response wasn't the result of how well I presented the cookies on a platter or how I looked in my baker's uniform...my business really began to grow.

Outlast the No's Until You Get to a Yes

Nobody makes a sale every time they make a presentation. Nobody.

Sometimes I'm amazed at who jumps in.

Sometimes I'm amazed at who doesn't.

I like a statement I read recently: "Just because you don't recognize a good business when you see one, doesn't mean you didn't see one."

Not everybody who sees a good idea really sees it.

Recognize, too that "to see" and "to seize" are two very different concepts. Many people see or hear a presentation, but they don't really see its potential in their life. Sometimes even those who see what might be don't follow through and seize the opportunity.

One week I had so many "no's" that I felt myself singing these lyrics to the tune of "Row, Row, Row Your Boat:"

No, no, no no no
No no no no no
No no no no no no no, no no no no YES!
No, no, no no no
No no no no no
No no no no no no no, no no no no YES!

The week hadn't been QUITE that bad, but at the moment it felt that bad. The good news was that eventually I had a YES.

A number of years ago, I watched a couple just keep persevering in their business. The economy around them was crumbling and various other factors seemed to be working against them, but they just kept making calls and presenting their business opportunity. Occasionally they got a "yes" response. Then one day they recruited a man to their business that really seemed to catch the vision. And then shortly after that, they recruited a second man who caught the vision. These two men ran with the business. They opened doors that had been locked tight, leaped over obstacles that seemed insurmountable, and made sales and recruited associates in a way that was truly phenomenal.

What happened to the couple that recruited these two men to their business? They received a tidy residual income each month based on the volume of sales of these two men!

Take a Positive Approach to Recruiting

Here are five very practical tips as you present your business to someone:

Tip 1: Ask for the Opportunity to "Bid"

If a person is reluctant to hear what you are offering as a business opportunity, try couching your request as an opportunity to bid. In essence, you are bidding on the way a person chooses to allocate their time and energy. You are offering an opportunity for a person to earn a significant amount of money—for THEIR discretionary use. You are offering a challenge.

Tip 2: Don't Give Too Much Information

Deal with the person at the level of information they have, and don't have. Too much information can be overwhelming. Lead a person along step by step.

Tip 3: Don't Push to Close

Rather than push for a decision, attempt to keep a person interested one more day. Keep feeding them information over time. Keep encouraging them to sample the products. Keep inviting them to seminars.

Tip 4: Don't Overstock a Person with Product

Don't insist that a person stock too much of your product at the outset. Most people who take on the whole load at the beginning feel overwhelmed. They are out a significant amount of cash as well as under a mountain of information to take in.

I always recommend to those in my particular business that they only sell a few basics to someone in the beginning. That's about all the average person can take in. Keep following up and keep building the arsenal of product and information that the recruit has...as the person progresses and as the person expresses interest and desire. You can't force a person to run with the business faster than that person wants to run, or is capable of running.

Tip 5: Start with What the Person Wants

Begin your conversation with what the other person wants...not what you want. Does she want financial freedom in three years? Does he want just a little relief in paying the bills?

If you are presenting your business to a couple, make sure you meet with both of them. Find out what they mutually want.

Work with them to develop a game plan so they can achieve what they want. It's only as you work within their dreams and goals that you truly will be able to help them.

You Just Never Know...

When I was growing up, our tradition was to go every Thanksgiving to my mother's family reunion that was held in the community where my mother grew up. My mother was the youngest of twelve children so there were more people at this reunion than you can imagine. For us, the trip meant a fairly long drive from Texas (where we lived) across Oklahoma and into Kansas (where most of the other family members lived). That was a long drive to make over Thanksgiving weekend, but the reunion was a priority for our family so we made the trip.

I always thought it was wonderful to see my cousins, even though I got a little weary of my older cousins always being held up to me as role models. One cousin in particular was introduced to me as, "This is your cousin who is planning to be a doctor." And later, "This is your cousin who is now studying to be a doctor." And later, "This is your cousin the doctor." And still later, "This is your cousin the ophthalmologist."

Not long ago, my cousin the ophthalmologist called me on the phone and guess what? He's now building a network marketing business! He entered the marketing business at the age of sixty-two.

Why did my cousin switch from medicine to direct sales? He realized a few years ago that there was neither the security nor the financial reward in his medical practice that there once had been. Many physicians in our nation are being bought out or undercut in their practices by HMO companies; others are struggling to pay very high malpractice insurance rates and increasingly high costs for equipment, facilities, and support staff. Physicians, however, nearly always enter their profession with some desire to serve, and many are increasingly frustrated that they are able to spend less and less time with their patients, even though they are charging them more and more per office visit.

My cousin discovered in a direct marketing business that he could truly serve people, make a difference in their lives, keep his overall business expenses to a minimum, and reap much greater financial rewards than he had enjoyed as an ophthalmologist. Furthermore, he didn't have to worry about being sued.

Physicians actually are accustomed to working very long hours and to doing what it takes to achieve a satisfactory outcome, so I have no doubt my cousin will be successful in his business. I can almost guarantee that he's going to feel just as fulfilled and have more fun!

One of the first people to really explain the direct-sales business to me was a physician. He made far more money than I did in a given year...but he also had great money needs.

One of the lessons I learned from this man is that people can be broke at different levels. He was working very hard for his salary. His expenses—especially his malpractice insurance expenses and medical equipment expenses—were astronomical. He had started a direct-sales business because being a doctor—a profession he dearly loved—just wasn't providing the financial rewards he desired for himself and his family.

Don't Over-Analyze or Over-Project

Don't over-analyze your direct-sales business. There's a lot to be said for just going with the flow of the business from day to day. The fact is, there's no real logic to why some people say "yes" to you—either to purchase your line of products or join you on the marketing side—and why others say "no." Some of the most likely people say "no" and of course, some of the least likely people say "yes." Sometimes you can present a truly dynamic presentation to a group and have very little response. At other times, you may feel as if you didn't do your very best and hit a homerun with a recruit who turns out to be a real go-getter.

Part of the reason you can't predict your success in any given appointment or meeting is because you don't know all that is going on in the lives of those to whom you are talking. In all likelihood, the person across from you at the café table or the person sitting in a meeting room has at least one reason for being present and interested in what you have to say, and also at least one reason for not being interested. Those reasons—the real, deep, core reasons—may be ones you can't discover in that particular appointment or meeting, and may be ones you will never fully uncover.

Never underestimate, however, the power of a person to lead you to a person to lead you to a person. You won't be able to predict that process.

You also won't be able to predict who will stick with the business in spite of very little initial success and who will leave the business at the first bout with discouragement.

You won't be able to predict how fast your business will grow. The good news is that your business will grow if you will continue to stick with the basics.

Stress Quality—and Do it Heartily.

Chapter 24
Build Up the People Around You

Let me share with you four basic, simple principles I have used in creating lasting business relationships. You likely have heard these principles before, but even so, you may be in a better place right now so that you truly can absorb these principles into your life and live them out. These are the foremost principles that people ignore, and as a result, they fail to succeed.

Principle 1: Vent No Negatives

It's very easy when we become a little discouraged in direct sales to vent our discouragement or voice every negative thing that happens to us. We tend to vent our problems or struggles to a spouse, a business associate, or a friend.

The expression of negatives doesn't do anybody any good— not even the person doing the venting. The person who hears the negatives is going to be discouraged or troubled— whatever momentum or positive joy they may have had in their day is going to vanish. The person who is doing the venting is going to have his negative attitude reinforced by hearing his own negative report!

"But I feel better if I vent," some people say in their own defense.

You may feel a little release of emotion or tension if you vent, but you don't really feel better. Ninety-nine times out of a hundred, you feel worse because you have given just that much extra time, energy, emotion, and expression to something that produces absolutely nothing toward building your business.

Remember always: Even if you have pain, you don't have to be a pain!

The only time to give time and energy to a negative situation, a problem, or a struggle is if you are actively seeking advice about how to change that situation, solve that problem, or overcome that struggle. When you couch a negative in those terms, it turns into a positive—it becomes a stepping-stone toward a better way of doing business.

The truth is, the vast majority of day-to-day problems, negative situations, or struggles blow over. They pass. Life moves on. It is only when you see a trend in problems or negative situations that you should even consider seeking advice about how to resolve or overcome them. Let the daily negative stuff of life roll right out of your mind and heart like water off the back of a duck.

Ask yourself, "Is what I'm about to say going to further my progress toward the next level up the ladder as I build my business?" If the answer is "no," "maybe," or "probably not"...keep your mouth shut.

There's an old saying: You can either be right or be happy. Many times people want to be right—they internalize certain circumstances, conversations, or encounters as being negative because somebody challenged their authority, ability, intelligence, or experience. What does it really matter if a person thinks you're right...or wrong? If you know that you have spoken the truth to the best of your ability, move on with your life! Don't let what another person says to you slow you down. Don't give their reaction to you any time or energy! Choose to be happy and positive and go on to the next moment in your day.

Principle 2: Check with Those Who Have Succeeded Before You

I've seen countless people make silly mistakes in their business because they forged ahead in a certain direction without first checking with their mentor.

The person who has gone before you to success...didn't get there by accident. That person knows things about your business that you don't yet know. Avail yourself of all the advice you can get from that person!

Your sponsor, mentor, or up-line supervisor can help you avoid pitfalls...detours...painful and costly mistakes. He or she can help you greatly to learn the ropes of your business.

When I began my business, it didn't matter one bit that I knew how to perform a Beethoven sonata. The level of expertise that I had in my old career didn't translate to my new career. That's true for most professions. Being a successful surgeon or contractor or automobile salesman doesn't necessarily mean that you know how to run a marketing network business. If you want to succeed in your new career, consult those who have already succeeded in it. Learn everything you can from your sponsor or up-line mentor.

Ask questions.

Listen to wise counsel.

Run your ideas and approaches by that person.

Don't reinvent the wheel. As you begin, go with what has been proven to produce results.

Principle 3: Be Generous in Your Words of Praise, Appreciation, and Encouragement

Don't embarrass anyone. Ridicule doesn't motivate. Neither does teasing a person about a poor lack of performance. The old saying is true: The subconscious doesn't take a joke.

Praise and appreciation do motivate. Choose to build up people. That certainly doesn't mean that you attempt to deify them. Make your words of praise and appreciation genuine and heartfelt. There's something about everybody that you can compliment. Find that something!

I once read a story about two junior officers in the Dutch navy. They agreed that any time they were in an officers club or in a setting with other members of the navy, they would talk positively about each other. They really set out to intentionally build each other up in the eyes of their peers and superiors. They did this faithfully. The two men became the two youngest admirals in the history of the Dutch navy. It wasn't until they both had been given their admiral rank that they admitted what they had set out to do: "Promote each other!"

What happens when you promote other people? Nine times out of ten, they, in turn, promote you. Good morale is built up on your team of associates. Your leadership is better respected—not only because of the good words that others say about you, but because of the good words you say about those who are under you. Everybody likes to work under a leader who is complimentary and generous with words of praise and appreciation. And ultimately, you are motivated and others are motivated to continue forward toward excellent service and high productivity.

If you want to move product...first move people with your uplifting words.

Principle 4: If You Are in Business With Your Spouse, Avoid Criticism of Your Spouse's Performance or Business Practices

So many times couples will attend motivational seminars or meetings and then on the way home, hit each other with a load of criticism.

"Did you hear what he said—he was speaking right to you!" "Well, she really nailed you in her presentation. I hope you were paying attention." "He was reading our resume when he said you should be doing..." "She must have been watching you. She sure knew that you don't..."

Maintaining a good relationship with your spouse as your business partner is vitally important to the success of your business. Agree together on your goals. Build up each other. Encourage each other.

Promote Others...And They Will Promote You

One of life's most basic relationship rules is this: You can't promote yourself. It doesn't matter who you are or what you have accomplished.

Oh, you can try. You can boast of all that you are and do, but all of your boasting will only make people turn away from you and respect you less. You can push and sell yourself with all you have, but all of your pushing and selling of self is far more likely to drive people away than it is to attract people.

The only way you can ultimately elevate yourself in the eyes of others is to promote other people.

The Person Who Puts Other People First Never Comes In Last.

Chapter 25
Choose to Lead

Most people in business, at some point, have been disappointed by somebody he or she just knew was going to make it BIG. They had high hopes for that person who seemed to have so much potential, so much enthusiasm, so many contacts, and such a great initial start.

All to no avail.

I had that happen to me just shortly before I was about to advance to a new level in my business. I went the third mile for this one particular person and his group. On the way after one meeting I thought, "They aren't going to make it." I didn't want that to be the truth, but it was and I had to face it.

I spent the next day feeling sorry for myself and very discouraged. A couple of other people had let me down. I was on the brink of advancing to a new level and was facing the very real possibility of failure at not achieving it. I felt very alone. It was just me and God.

I don't mind telling you that, in retrospect, "me and God" is a pretty good place to be.

About five o'clock the next morning, I went into the bathroom of the hotel where my daughter and I had spent the night. I took my little notepad with me, and for the next hour or so, I rewrote my personal and business goals. I wrote a couple of letters. I decided that I couldn't give more time and effort to the people I had hoped would produce but weren't producing. I needed to refocus my efforts in another direction. I pulled my group together the next week and said to them, "I'm going to reach this goal! Who's going with me to the next level?"

The fire and enthusiasm that broke out in that group was tremendous. Momentum took hold and never stopped until the goal was reached.

It was in that week that I truly began to lead. Up to that time, I had been just one of the group—enjoying the fellowship, being pals with everybody, encouraging as much as

---

I could. That week I stepped up to the plate and said, "Enough floating on calm water. Let's paddle this boat and take it somewhere!"

The entire group rose with me—each person or couple to the next rung of the ladder. We began to work together as a team.

Guess what happened? The organization for which I had such high hopes didn't like it at all that other groups were starting to overtake their position. They got in gear and who knows, they may still make it!

When you place high expectations on one particular person or group in your organizations, several things happen—none of them good. You subconsciously begin to put pressure on that person or group. You may not say anything that sounds like pressure to you, but your body language and the set of your jaw will give a signal of pressure to what it is that you do say. People rarely respond to pressure. They perceive it as threatening or negative, and they tend to have a negative reaction to it—they may walk away, cower in fear, withdraw from you personally, or just plain quit.

You'll feel much freer in giving encouragement and imparting genuine enthusiasm and appreciation if you will always have a back-up person who is producing for you, and then a couple of spares beyond that. Don't limit yourself to one or two people on whom you pin all your hopes. Build a team.

Choose to Teach

Every direct-sales organization that I know involves teaching. Teaching is a form of leading.

Furthermore, every successful direct-sales person I know has made teaching a priority. Teaching is at the heart of duplication, and that's the primary way a direct-sales business grows. Selling involves products. Teaching involves the people who sell products, and who in turn, recruit and teach others. The cycle is pretty much the same: sell and recruit...teach and inspire...sell and recruit...teach and inspire...and so forth.

Imagine that an associate of yours comes to you and say, "Please come help me make a presentation. This new guy under me has invited fifteen outstanding prospects to his home for an evening to discuss our business. They are all interested and seem eager to learn more. Please come and talk to them!"

Well, of course you are eager to go! You get all of your materials together and are excited about this opportunity.

Then you set foot in house and meet the man who has invited these fifteen people to his home. You look around. There are no chairs set up and no refreshments prepared for the people who are about to come to the meeting. It dawns on you that you have not done an adequate job of training this associate in how to set up a presentation.

Three people show up. One is a neighbor who comes to the meeting in her house slippers. Another is a man who quickly admits that he's there because his boss at work told him he had to come. The third guy doesn't say much.

What do you do and say in that moment?

Your immediate instinct is probably to say, "These aren't the people I'm after" and run for the hills!

What you actually do and say in that moment is going to be a mark of your leadership. Do you give the presentation your best effort?

A real leader will present his information as if he's speaking in an elegant home to two dozen of the sharpest people in the community. A real leader will do his best to edify the man who hosted the evening.

Edification is not deification. Some people get confused on that point. To edify means to build up someone or to promote them. It doesn't mean to exalt them to the point of worship.

To edify means to encourage a person, and one of the most encouraging things you can do is to teach a person how to be more successful. To promote a person doesn't just mean you identify all of their accomplishments and take note of their engaging personality and great potential and intelligent demeanor. To promote a person means that you do what you can to help that person advance, and some times that means telling the person how to dress, how to entertain, how to set up a business environment, and even how to set up chairs in a room.

Choose to Challenge

A leader or a teacher always challenges his followers or students to take a next, bold step.

I recently challenged my team to distribute five tapes a week. These are introductory tapes about the product line I sell and the opportunity to become involved in the business. Now, I didn't challenge my team to buy five new tapes a week and give them away. I challenged those on my team to distribute five tapes—to loan them out, retrieve them, follow through with the people to whom they loaned the tapes, and then distribute those same tapes the next week to five different people. Almost immediately, business began to grow rapidly for all of those who made this commitment.

If a person hasn't listened to the tape within a week, ask the person to do the courtesy of returning the tape to you. This sends a signal that you aren't just playing...you are running a business and what you are doing is important to you.

I never encourage people to give away tapes or promotional materials. That lessens the value of the tapes or packet. Rather, I encourage people to loan tapes and promotional items. At the time the loan is made, set up time for retrieving what you are loaning. Say simply, "Can I come by next Thursday and pick up this material?" If Thursday isn't good for the person, find a time that is!

That way, when you go to pick up the material, if the person has any interest whatsoever, you have another opportunity to present your plan or product line (in just ten minutes or less), and another opportunity to loan yet another tape to the person. This keeps the relationship alive!

The results of my five-tapes-a-week challenge were explosive, not only in my business but in the lives of every person who took that challenge! Many of them, in turn, challenged those they were leading or teaching. The results multiplied very quickly.

Get to Know Your Team Members

If you sponsor a person, really get to know that person. Find out what motivates them, what goals and dreams they are pursuing, and a little bit about the disappointments they may have had in their life. It's also important, I believe, for you to discover what it is that they will have to lay aside to really succeed in your business.

I entered the direct-sales business thinking that I was something of a high-achiever. I had a little bit of evidence to back that up. I had been chosen Who's Who in American Colleges and Universities—twice. One year I was selected as an "Outstanding Young Woman in California" for my music accomplishments.

When a person who is an achiever begins a network marketing business, that person starts at the bottom. It doesn't matter if the person was surgeon general, a well-respected attorney, a real-estate whiz kid, or an academic dean. It is humbling—and sometimes irritating, frustrating, disappointing, discouraging, and painful—for a person to lay aside their past achievements and, in essence, start over to build a new reputation based upon a new criteria of expectations and challenges.

Also find out what the person doesn't know. Many people who enter direct-sales businesses have very little experience in sales, per se. They may have been teachers, administrators, assistants, or clerical support staff. They may have been in a respected profession such as law or medicine. They may have been in sports or in the entertainment industry. They have to lay aside what they know how to do and learn something they have never thought about doing before. Some willingly embrace the concepts of salesmanship, others seem to be naturals without much training, and others have to learn from the ground up how_to make a presentation, how to close a deal, and how to set up an appointment by phone. Some take all this on as great adventure and challenge; others struggle. And it's OK to struggle—those who struggle will make it if they just keep on struggling and don't give up.

Listen, listen, listen. Calvin Coolidge once said, "No man ever listened himself out of a job."

Listening is one of the most valuable skills you'll ever develop. It is the key to learning things about a person you can learn through no other means.

People can read themselves into a job...talk themselves into a job...and behave themselves into a job. But if you want to develop a relationship with someone and sustain that relationship over time, you have to listen.

People can talk themselves out of a job and behave themselves out of a job. People who truly listen and then respond appropriately to others are people whose presence is always welcome...yes, even highly valued.

Seek Out Ways to Help and Serve

Notice what people around you need. I once was involved in a music festival in Prague—it was a beautiful auditorium and I didn't want to leave, not even to get a drink. My throat became quite dry. One young woman from Prague came up to me and handed me her coin purse. She didn't speak English but she motioned with her hands so that I knew she wanted me to go and use the coins in her purse to get something to drink. I did, and later paid her back.

I couldn't help but think, "How kind, and how perceptive, of that young woman to see what I needed and to make a move to meet that need." She hadn't been afraid to take the risk involved in reaching out to someone who didn't speak her language and didn't know where the beverages were located, much less someone who seemed to have greater authority in the situation than she had. She saw a need and moved to meet it. I was very grateful and I've never forgotten her.

People will be thankful that you moved to meet a need in their lives, too—they won't forget you.

Think of the Phone as Your Encouragement Link

The starting block for a network marketing business is the telephone. Every person I know who has succeeded in a direct-sales business spends about half of their work time on the phone. Initially, much of that time is spent in making calls to set up appointments and invite people to meetings. Later, the bulk of the time is spent encouraging those who may be disheartened, answering questions, giving practical advice, and maintaining a high level of morale and motivation among the various members of your team.

One of the most powerful questions you can ask is, "What can I do to help you?" Or, "How can I assist you?"

As you make contact with those on your team regularly, you are sending a strong message, "I'm here for you. I want you to succeed. I believe you can succeed."

Every person who is in a self-operated business faces a mountain of reasons not to build their business. The nagging or negative spouse. The demands of a full-time job. The personal and family problems every person encounters from time to time. The troubles of the world at large. It's a good feeling to know there's somebody who believes in you and wants to see you become all you can become and earn all you can earn!

Develop A "Complimentary" Attitude

As a teacher, a large part of my job was to evaluate students—to evaluate their voices for choirs and ensembles, to correct musical errors in preparations for performance, and to give tests and grades. For a number of years, I traveled fairly extensively adjudicating choirs—more evaluating and judging. I had to learn in my direct-sales business to not judge or give critical comments.

Many people fire away with cutting remarks and then say, "Oh, I was just teasing" or "I was just joking." Not really. Teasing and cutting jokes usually have a foundation of truth.

Furthermore, the person who is the recipient of that negative teasing or joke isn't likely to think what they are hearing is fun. They may be hurt to the core. Unless you really know a person and know with certainty that they also will think what you are saying is funny or in pure jest, keep your mouth shut.

If you believe you have hurt someone's feelings, don't delay in writing that person a note of apology or picking up the phone and saying, "I'm truly sorry for what I said. I value you as a person and I was out of line in saying what I said."

Rather than allow yourself to fall into a critical mode, choose instead to become a frequent giver of compliments. If someone is working hard, let that person know that you appreciate their effort and that you admire their diligence. If someone shows a caring attitude, thank them for their concern and service.

Be quick to say

❖ "Thank you."
❖ "You look great."
❖ "You did a good job."

Let people know they are special...they are appreciated...they are valued.

When my daughter was a teenager I learned that girls have just as big an appetite as boys! They want to look their best—from just the right hairstyle and eye makeup to just the right shoes. They want to have all the boys admire them, even if they don't really want to date any of them. And they don't care at all who sees them eat what.

Years ago I took all of my daughter's basketball team out for dinner after a game. We laughed and talked and ate. One of the girls wrote, "Thanks a lot for the dinner. It was great. I enjoyed talking to you about music and voice lessons. I think you're neat."

What a special note that was to me! Do you remember how special it was when you were a teenager to have an adult believe in you and encourage you and support you, even when your team might have been losing or you may not have done your best on stage?

Choose today to be the person who makes someone else feel special.

Replace Criticism With Applause

As far as I am concerned, there is no such thing as constructive criticism. All criticism is destructive at some level, and especially in the intent of the person who makes the critical remark. If a person gives you advice, that can be constructive. But if a person says, "Wow, what happened to your hair today—it didn't cooperate with your comb did it?" or, "Are you still driving that old Dodge?" the feeling you have deep inside isn't good. You feel put down and negative—not only about yourself but about the person who made the comment.

One of the worst ways you can hurt a person is to sandwich negative criticism between two compliments. The critical comment will stand out and sting all the more. For example: "You did a great job in your presentation, but you went really long. It kinda got boring there in the middle. But you finished strong!" The recipient of this criticism sandwich won't know where he or she stands with you, and be less inclined to want to hear what you have to say in the future. The best approach is to avoid the criticism altogether.

If there's something you believe will help your spouse or a person you have sponsored, make your suggestion before the person prepares or delivers his next presentation. Don't hit the person with the advice right after they've finished a presentation. For example: "As you are getting ready for tomorrow night's presentation, you might want to consider shortening the middle part of your presentation. That would leave more time for people to ask questions at the end." That's advice a person can consider without feeling the sting of criticism.

Be Grateful for the Strong-Willed, Self-Motivated Person

I grew up in Texas...and I just kept growing up and growing up in Texas. By the time I was in fifth grade, I was as tall as the teacher—and the way I acted, some people thought I was the teacher.

Let me encourage you today—if you have a strong-willed child, take hope. If you can get that child trained by saying "no" enough times, that child can do great things.

One day I forgot my coat. My teacher loaned me her coat, which was a very nice coat. Her husband was an oilman and she had gone back to teaching school just for something to do during the day. Of course, the teacher didn't know she had loaned me her coat. I simply went into the cloakroom and took her coat off the hook, and that day, I wore a full-length mink coat out on the playground to play kickball!

About a month later, I was invited by a boy to go to a birthday party. Even more amazing was the fact that this boy was as tall as I was, and at the party, he asked me to dance! I went to a very strict church and we didn't dance or do anything fun. I thought, "This is my one and only chance to dance in my whole life." We danced the two-step to the song "Long, Long Ago" and I decided that I liked dancing a great deal.

The next day at school when the teacher took all of the kids out to recess, I stayed behind in the classroom with the teacher's permission. While everybody was gone, I took it upon myself to push all of the desks to the edges of the room. When the teacher returned she asked, "Beverly, what's this?" I said, "We're going to have a dance!" She said, "Do you mind if we have spelling first?" I replied, "That will be OK. You have spelling and I'll go get everything ready for the dance."

I went down to the principal's office, called the "room mother," and told her that we needed soft drinks, cookies, and a record player and records. And I quickly added, "And don't forget that song 'Long Long Ago.'" I'm a little amazed now to look back and realize that the room mother actually showed up with those things by the time spelling was over...and for the rest of the day, we had a dance!

If my father had known about all this, of course, I wouldn't be alive today.

I'm telling you all of this to say: If you have somebody working with you in a sales organization who shows the same tendencies that I had as a fifth grader...don't be dismayed. Be glad! You may need to call give person wise counsel from time to time, but never ever try to diminish their enthusiasm or their take-charge attitude. It's much better to have someone who is self-motivated and strong-willed than to have someone in your organization that you continually need to jump start like a dead battery on a cold morning.

Orchestrate A Quality Team Effort

An orchestra sounds like chaos when the various members begin warming up before a performance. The sound can actually be so disharmonious and nerve-grating that an audience member just might be tempted to flee the auditorium.

But then a pitch is played against which all other orchestra members are required to tune their instruments. Even then, the noise that comes from the stage is just that—so much NOISE.

Finally, the conductor takes the stand and the first downbeat is given. What has sounded like so much noise up to that point, suddenly bursts into...well, music! Assuming of course that the orchestra has quality musicians in it, the music has a clearly discernable rhythm and cadence...harmonious melodic lines...musical themes and movements...and tremendous full-orchestra sounds interspersed with sterling solo segments.

In many ways, network marketing bears the same protocol as an orchestra preparing for performance. If every person in the larger organization just does his own thing, the result is chaos. If every person conducts his business without using the tried-and-proven systems and tools provided by the corporation, the result is less than perfect. But if every person follows the prescribed protocol, uses the tools and systems as they were designed to be used, gives accurate information, makes an agreed-upon number of calls and hosts an ideal number of meetings...the entire team moves forward in a way that results in tremendous success for every person on the team. People working together toward the same goal and using the same methods always results in a greater success than individuals marching to their own drummer.

Choose to lead.

Forget Notoriety. Lead and Build With Humility.

Chapter 26
Stay Connected

A network marketing business is not a Lone Ranger business. Rather, it's a "posse" business. No person truly becomes successful in a direct-sales business all on his or her own. Those who rise to the top do so because they have built a team of people who are motivated to pursue a common goal.

It is vitally important that you stay connected to your team. People who jump from one group to another, from one idea to another, or from one project to another rarely succeed. Stay focused and stay connected.

Let me give you a few tips:

❖ Don't Play a Blame Game. Someplace along the line you may feel like blaming somebody else for your lack of success:

"I have the wrong sponsor..."
"I'm in the wrong group..."
"I was assigned to the wrong team..."
"My father never loved me..."
"My mother never taught me how to work..."

Stop the blame game. You're only hindering your own forward progress.

❖ Learn from Your Sponsor or Mentor. Always listen to the voice of experience. There is someone who knows more about your business than you know. He or she can provide invaluable counsel as to what to do, when, and how. Listen and learn. Be able to take constructive and helpful advice from others.

As I have already stated, I don't believe there is such a thing as "constructive criticism." Those two words don't belong in the same phrase as far as I am concerned. Either you are constructive in what you say to another person—helpful and encouraging as you attempt to build up the person and train them to improve their performance, always with an eye toward their succeeding—or you are critical, which nearly always tends to tear down a person and discourage him.

Never dish out criticism. But if you believe criticism has been dished out to you, search through that load of criticism to find the one nugget that might help you. If you'll do that, you can turn the negative words you've received into a positive idea.

I used to give singing lessons and one of the most difficult things about teaching singing is this: The person nearly always takes a critical comment about their voice quality or performance as a criticism of their total person. Very few people are automatically objective about their voice. The same is true for business performance. Many people take all constructive advice personally. If you truly want to benefit from what others attempt to teach you, be objective about your work performance and be open to suggestions about the way you can improve your presentations and conduct your business.

If a mentor is attempting to help you overcome some obstacles or increase your performance, listen to what he says. Don't let your feelings get in the way. Hear specifically what he recommends. Ask, "How can I do that?" and "Is there anything else you can tell me that will help me succeed?" A person who is a willing learner is a person who is likely to succeed at a quick pace.

❖ Don't Reinvent the Wheel. Find out what others have done and how they've accomplished their goals. Ask questions.

Ask what level of success other people have had when they invested the amount of hours you are planning to invest in your business the first year.

Don't try to reinvent the wheel. Find out what has worked repeatedly and over time for others.

In addition, you have to stay up with the trends. Don't be left behind when it comes to the latest information and inspiration provided by those in leadership.

Stick With the Tried-and-Proven

Years ago I went snorkeling in Bora-Bora. The coral there has incredibly vibrant colors and it truly is a beautiful experience to see it. We were told by the hotel staff that we needed to wear plastic shoes while we were snorkeling because the coral is also extremely sharp. As a group of us were following our guide out to the coral, we were in about five feet of water when our guide stopped and unfurled a long yellow cord. He told us to hold onto it, and he motioned for us to put our face masks down into the water. Then this guide proceeded to throw huge pieces of red meat into the water.

Within seconds, we were surrounded by about fifty sharks in a variety of sizes and shapes!

I don't mind telling you that I experienced immediate feelings of panic. I couldn't help thinking, "These sharks are in the water with me! There's no glass between me and the sharp, flesh-ripping teeth of these fish! I'm just holding onto this stupid yellow cord."

What the guide had told us was this: "Stand still and hold the line! If you let go and try to get away, a shark will come after you. But if you stand still, the sharks will come right toward you and then veer away when they see you aren't moving. Stay together and hold the line!"

It took everything within me to stand still and not try to out-swim those sharks. But I believed what the guide said more than I trusted in my own fear. I held onto that cord and sure enough, the sharks would swim toward me, then veer away at what seemed like the last second.

Stick with your team and your game plan. Don't jump lines. Don't get off the system and try to do your own thing. Stay tight with your line.

After about five minutes, the sharks finished eating all the meat that had been thrown into the water. The blood in the water dissipated. The sharks wandered off. Eventually, we all walked back toward the wooden boat that had brought us to the place.

Would I repeat that experience? No way. Am I glad I did it once so I could brag to my children about it? Absolutely.

I feel the same way about the early years in my business. Do I want to go back and redo those years? No way. Am I glad I worked as hard and long as I did? Am I glad I stuck with my team and didn't let go of the lifeline I was thrown? Am I glad I didn't try to do it "my way" but rather, did it the "tried and proven way?"

I don't have a shred of doubt as I shout a loud "yes" to each of those last three questions!

Wisdom is Found in the Counsel of the Wise.

PART VI

Positive Success

Chapter 27
Choose to Make a Positive Difference

As a music student—and later as a music teacher—I always seemed to be memorizing the dates of various composer's lives.

Bach — 1685–1750
Mozart — 1756–1791
And so forth.

One day as I was reflecting on this, the thought occurred to me—there's a lot left unsaid in that dash between the year of birth and the year of death. There's a lifetime in each of those dashes!

It's not when a person is born or dies that matters very much in the long run, even though that's what we put on a person's tombstone. It's the life that was lived in the dash.

What kind of life do you want to live?

What of your life do you want to leave behind as a legacy?

What will your life have stood for...counted for...been lived for?

Act With a Positive Purpose

Do you remember when you were younger and people asked you if you did something by accident or on purpose. One of my foremost goals is to do everything I do on purpose.

I go to places on purpose.

I meet with people on purpose.

I make phone calls on purpose.

My purpose is to make friends, influence people for good, sell product, recruit people to my business, and be a person of genuine integrity, faith, and a strong commitment to the best of values.

There's an old song that said: "I want to live fast, love hard, die young, and leave a beautiful memory."

I've adapted that lyric this way: "I want to live swift, work hard, die wealthy, and leave many people debt free."

Help Other People's Dreams Come True

A reporter once asked me, "Beverly, what really makes you tick?"

This person had followed me around for a couple of days—going with me to some of my favorite shops and restaurants. He had walked on the beach with me and enjoyed the view from my penthouse apartment. He sensed, however, that there was more to me than shopping and fine dining—I'm so glad he sensed that!

I said in response to the reporter, "Come with me."

We drove north to downtown Los Angeles—the heart of the city that many people never see. We went to 30th and Grand to Rosey Grier's "Are You Committed?" Project.

While we were there, Tracy came in. I first met Tracy when he went to the center at nineteen years old to learn his ABC's. He hadn't gone to school. No...Tracy wasn't raised in Africa. He was raised in Los Angeles, but he managed to bypass the L.A. school system. Meeting Tracy really touched my teacher's heart. I became a strong supporter of the "Are You Committed?" project.

I know other business people who have had their heart-strings tugged by other causes and concerns. One person's heart broke when he went to a cerebral palsy center. Another couple's hearts went out to those who were diagnosed with HIV and AIDS. One woman's heart-strings were pulled when she saw mentally deficient children born to crack cocaine users.

There's some place where you are needed. Follow your heart.

When Tracy came in, he was wearing a Jesus sweatshirt and carrying a can of chili, which was his food for the day. I asked Rosey if we could take video footage of Tracy and Ben, his teacher. Rosey agreed and so did the young men. What a joy to my heart as I saw Ben teaching Tracy to read out of the Bible because that's the book Tracy wanted to learn to read!

Care Enough to be Willing to Act

Years ago I was sitting in a Bible study with some good friends of mine and we began to discuss the question, "How can we be of greater service to our community?" It's one thing to go to church and hear about loving others—it's another thing to apply that message in everyday circumstances and meet practical needs in the community where we live.

One of the people in the group whose name was Vic, a physician, said, "Well, I can tell you one thing we could do for starters. I was just paged by my office. I have an alcoholic patient who has just spun out of control and is in a rage. I need to go to her. Anybody want to come with me?"

We looked at each other as if to say, "You mean, now? You mean, be of service right this instant?"

We went.

We walked into a small, unpainted house that had very little furniture and bare floors. We found this woman ranting and raving. Both of her legs had been amputated as a consequence of diabetes, so as she was ranting and raving, she was scooting herself around on the floor. Her daughter, thirteen years old, was hiding in a bedroom in fear, curled up on a mattress that had no sheets, no pillow, and no blanket. I thought to myself, "Are we still in America? How can this mother and her daughter live in conditions like this?"

Dr. Vic showed us how to calm this woman. I began to work with various volunteers to get some food and furniture into that house. We organized a work party to paint the house and then helped this woman to get into a rehab program and, later, to get a job.

Our going to that woman's home that night was a tremendous risk.

None of us felt qualified to be there.

None of us really knew what to do.

But we cared.

We were willing to do something.

And those two ingredients—caring and being willing to act—are often all it takes to get something started, to help something grow, and to motivate someone near to you to be and do more than they have ever thought they could be or do.

I've watched this pattern repeat itself a number of times through the years: Caring, and a willingness to act, changes individual lives and ultimately, is the combination that builds strong, vibrant, make-a-difference organizations.

Moving Beyond Yourself

The first obligation you have is to pay your own bills. After that, see what cause captures your heart.

I talked to a person not long ago who had reached a degree of success in his business. He said, "I've got enough. There's nothing more I really want or need. Why should I continue to work hard or set goals to reach a higher level?"

I said, "You may have everything you need or desire, but have you looked around? There are lots of people who don't have anything. They are far from having their needs met, much less their desires. Work to help them."

He said, "Like what?"

I said, "If you're serious, I can give you names and addresses for ten projects that need your help. If you want a reason to build your business, I can give you a reason!"

He said, "Name just one."

I said, "Did you know that there's an organization that sponsors the children who were heavily radiated as a result of the Chernobyl nuclear disaster to go to England where they receive a therapeutic experience that emphasizes clean water, clean air, and nutritious food? This therapy has been found to add two QUALITY years, on average, to the life of these children."

He said, "I'll take it on!"

The Joy of Giving Generously

I went to Los Angeles several years ago to present a check on behalf of my corporation to a local charity. The specific project had been a Bowl-a-Thon and I was there to give a check of about $350,000. I heard a voice timidly ask, "Beverly, is that you?"

It was one of my Kansas cousins! She had worked hard in raising contribution money for the Bowl-a-Thon and had a check of a couple thousand dollars to give. She was amazed at the size of the gift I was there to present on behalf of my corporation.

Now, I am not in the least denigrating the size of the contribution my cousin was making. She had been soliciting contributions from people who don't make a great deal of money and therefore, they couldn't give a great deal of money.

What I am very pleased about is that I work in a business that allows me to make a lot of money so I can give a lot of money. I'm grateful that our organization is very prosperous and it has an entire division devoted to making contributions to meaningful projects that build up communities.

Being prosperous in business should always result in generosity to those in need. Those who make a lot of money certainly can afford life's luxuries and they should suffer no penalty for enjoying them. But those who make a lot of money also have the added joy of being able to contribute generously to worthy causes for the betterment of individuals and groups of people who are in great need. Making a lot of money should never be a matter of I-have-it-and-you-don't. Rather, it should be a matter of helping raise the water level of an entire community.

Some people seem satisfied with very little. I'm not one of them.

Some people seem to have no goals of bettering their lifestyle or enjoying the finest life has to offer. I'm not one of them.

Some people seem to have no ambition or desire to help others in any way that is beyond their current means of providing encouragement and provision. I'm not one of them.

I have big aspirations, big goals, and a big desire to make a positive difference. I want to see students from other nations who have musical ability have an opportunity to study and reach their potential. I want to see people in India who have no access to a hospital receive the medical care they desperately need. I want to see college students turned onto the idea of free enterprise and be equipped to step up to the plate to move our nation forward so that we, as the American people, can continue to give our creativity, ideas, products, and life-enhancing services to those who are less fortunate around the world.

How big are your dreams for helping other people?

I encourage you to dream big and make a difference in our world that is in desperate need of a positive change!

Open Your Heart to Take On a Need. Then Open Your Wallet, Your Schedule, Your Energy, and Your Creativity. Let's Make a Difference!

Chapter 28
Enjoy the Rewards

I wanted to learn to scuba dive in the worst way, but I was a little scared even though I'm a strong swimmer. I didn't want anybody to know I was scared so I went to Maui for three weeks, holed up in a little hideaway, chartered a boat and a scuba instructor, and said, "I want to learn to scuba dive."

Within a week I was certified! I was very proud of myself!

Several months later, I went to a convention in an area known for it's beautiful scuba environments. One afternoon, several people said, "What do you want to do? We have some time off—where shall we go?"

I said, "I want to scuba dive."

A diver who had seen me dive the day before said, "Come with me. I'm going to show you something very special."

I followed him into the water and we dove down about seventy feet. He had told me in advance what to expect. He said, "I'm going to take you to a place called The Cathedrals. There's an opening about five feet in diameter. The surge will be tremendous but hold on to me and I'll tell you when to go through." Just when the tide was right, he pushed me through the hole. He was right—the surge was tremendous. As I emerged from that small opening, I found myself in a chamber with unbelievably beautiful coral formations and shafts of light coming all that way down to them. It truly was like being in a mystical, magical cathedral. It was one of the most beautiful sights I've ever seen. The effort of pushing through the tidal surge paled in comparison to the joy of seeing what I saw that day.

After you have made the effort to push through the difficult and intense stages of a network marketing business, you will likely feel that the rewards are greater in comparison to the effort you put out.

Having Sufficient Money is Fun!

I've been without money and I've had money and trust me, having money is a lot more fun.

Did you ever experience a holiday season in which you did not receive the gift you wanted?

I distinctly remember the Christmas in which everybody decided that I was too grown up for dolls...and I got socks and underwear instead. I may have been grown-up in their minds, but trust me, I still wanted a doll for Christmas!

I'm not sure anybody ever gets beyond the point where they want house shoes or ties instead of toys.

Part of the joy of getting BEYOND the point of being able to pay your bills is being able to have FUN doing some things that you once thought of as being extravagant.

Never Let It Fade Away....

I love coats with pockets, perhaps because one of my favorite songs is "Catch a Falling Star." And what do you do with a falling star according to the song? You put it in your pocket and never let it fade away!

Have you ever put on a coat that you haven't worn for awhile and reached into a pocket and pulled out something you had forgotten you had put into your pocket? The item you discovered probably evoked a memory.

Recently I put on a coat and found all sorts of little mementos of the previous year in its pockets...

There was a ticket stub to *Phantom of the Opera*—I saw it three times one year because I loved it so much. The ticket was for the second row. There was also a ticket stub for *Black and Blue*, a musical that I saw four times.

There was the business card of the manager of the L'Escada store located on Avenue Montagne in Paris. As far as I'm concerned, L'Escada produces the most fabulous, beautiful, and expensive line of clothes in the world—what fun I had shopping there in April!

There was a card from the Hotel Mayorasco on the Spanish island of Palma Majorca. The beautiful bays with their fishing boats bobbing on the bright blue water, white-washed buildings with red tile roofs overshadowed by a beautiful thirteenth-century cathedral—it's an absolutely wonderful island on which to unwind.

There was a little scrap of paper on which I had written the address of a church. Those who know me well know that one of my favorite things to do is read the *New York Times* over a tall latte. One Sunday after a wonderful week in the Big Apple, I read in the paper about a world-renowned boy's choir that was scheduled to sing at St. Thomas Episcopal Church on 5th Avenue. I decided to go hear that choir. I stepped through the large doors of that cathedral and immediately found myself far away from the hustle and bustle of the city. I sank down in a pew and let the sun streaming through the stained glass windows bathe me in its patterns of colored light. I closed my eyes and let the angelic-sounding music of these fifty or so boys seep deep into my soul. It was a glorious experience.

I also found in my pocket a thousand pesetas and a ten-thousand lire note. They brought back memories of being at the Vatican in Rome. While touring, we encountered a group of German tourists and when I overheard enough of their conversations to realize they were about to have a private audience with the Pope, I said to my traveling companion, "Let's just blend in with the group!" We sat about fifty feet from the Pope. As he spoke, we realized that the people in that group had grown up in Eastern Europe—in nations that until just two decades ago had been under communist domination. They felt truly blessed to be able to travel abroad and to experience genuine religious freedom.

There was a business card from a limo driver and a phone card for use of public telephones in France. There was a napkin from a café in the Dolder Grand Hotel in Zurich, which looks like a palace. It's a hundred years old, located high above the city overlooking the lake and a golf course—it's accessible by a cable car. We went to tea in the afternoon and an opera at night.

There was a matchbook from a thatched-roof hotel in Bora-Bora. I had a hammock, two palm trees, and a book to read one afternoon. A few yards away was a beautiful beach and the ocean beyond—with fabulous snorkeling—and occasionally a waitress would come by and ask me if I wanted anything to drink.

There was a little piece of ribbon that had been tied around a small box of exquisite chocolates. I ate all the chocolates in that box while sitting in a church one morning—I'd never eaten chocolates in church before.

There was a tiny toothbrush from the ladies' lounge at the Palace Hotel in New York City. By every sink in the ladies' lounge there, you'll find a toothbrush and a small bottle of hand lotion. Several of my friends and I enjoyed an elegant tea there in the Gold Room—we felt like queens as we listened to the harpist and enjoyed the delicacies we were served.

There was a card with the name of James Bachman. I had attended a concert at Carnegie Hall. About ten preteen black and Hispanic boys filed in to sit next to me. With them was an older man. I quickly determined that the man must a teacher and the boys were his students. At the intermission, I asked the boy sitting next to me, "Are you here with your music teacher?" He said, "No, ma'am. He's our choir director. We are part of the New Amsterdam Boy's Choir from Brooklyn. My name is Tyler. What's your name?" I told him my name. The boy next to him piped up, "My name is Jason." Both boys were the epitome of politeness. I whispered, "How did you get the tickets to this concert?" They said, "Our director got them for us." I introduced myself to the choir director and he told me that he routinely approached businesses to see if they would sponsor some of his boys to attend concerts such as the one we were at. I handed him two hundred dollars and said, "Take them out to pizza after the concert!" How wonderful to be able to do that!

There were some French francs. They reminded me of going to the Orsay Museum of impressionist art in Paris and then to Montmarte, where we enjoyed freshly baked bread and the newly created art pieces sold on the streets by local residents.

There was also the eighth-grade graduation program for my son Paul. He received the art award and was on the Honor Roll. At the end of the ceremony, the graduates stood and sang for their mothers, "You Are the Wind Beneath My Wings." Paul gave me a long-stemmed red rose and said, "Thanks, Mom, for always being there for me."

These bits of memory from my coats are very special to me. They are the falling stars that I once had as only a far-away dream. They are reminders of the dreams that kept me motivated while I was packing boxes of product at three o'clock in the morning, shrugging off the "no's," smiling when I didn't feel like smiling, and making a presentation when I hardly had the energy to stand.

And oh, there is one more thing I always find in my purses or coat pockets—a tape to encourage people to be a business owner. I never go anywhere without a tape to pass along.

Hold on to your dreams. And do what it takes to turn them into a reality! One of the great joys of doing well in your business is having opportunities for fun with friends and family members.

Enjoy!

Take Time to Smell the Roses You've Planted and Grown in Your Own Garden of Success!

"Choosing the positive" is just that – a <u>choice</u>. Many people seem to have a built-in tendency toward the negative. Our society criticizes readily – performances, appearances, behavior, and political decisions and results. News and editorial opinions are geared toward the negative, the problematic, the disastrous, and the downward trend. We are bombarded daily with countless commercial messages about what is wrong and therefore, what needs to be fixed, adjusted, changed, replaced, or renewed. Staying positive requires that we make a personal decision to choose the positive.

Nobody can make the choice to be positive but you. The responsibility is yours and yours alone. Nobody else can make you into a positive person.

The good news is, you can make that choice! No matter how bleak the circumstances, how trying the relationship, how difficult the situation, or how pessimistic the prevailing opinion, you can decide within yourself that you will be establish a consistently different trend, create a different atmosphere, and establish a different foundation for personal success.

You can choose to become positively directed and try something new in your life.

You can choose to become positively prepared so that you are "ahead of the curve" instead of playing catch-up.

You can choose to be positively committed toward reaching your goals.

You can choose to be positively motivated, guarding closely what you allow into your mind and out of your own mouth.

You can choose to be positively linked to other people as you build a team and stay connected with those who are pursuing your same goals.

You can choose to make a positive difference and enjoy your own life.

The choice for the positive is a daily choice. Nobody awakens every morning feeling on top of the world. But every person can go to bed each night believing that he or she has done something to further their own success and the success of others.

You can become a positive charge in a negative world.

Will you step up to the challenge?

I have a positive hope that you will!

About the Author

Beverly Sallee is an internationally recognized business woman, inspirational speaker, musician, and philanthropist.

Beverly holds a bachelor of arts degree in piano and a master of arts degree in choral conducting. In 1978, she found herself at a cross-roads in her life. She had been teaching at the university level for ten years, and was struggling to juggle her commitments as a wife, mother, student, piano teacher, choral conductor, music professor, and volunteer—but she felt herself at a dead-end financially. With a strong desire to give her children a better life and an excellent education, she began a part-time direct-marketing business. Her entrepreneurial business grew dramatically and successfully, and by 1985, she had achieved a level that allowed her to leave her university position and pursue her business full-time.

Today, Beverly's business has expanded to forty-nine nations. She continues her passion for music by giving music scholarships all over the world through the Oregon Bach Festival and Stuttgart Bachakademie Germany. She continues to work with Easter Seals on the national level. She is helping build a hospital in Calcutta, India and is active in the Network of Caring established in association with World Vision.

Beverly's motto is "the world is my home and the sky is the limit." She invites you to give your life a positive charge – to soar, professionally and personally – and to join her in the first-class echelon of the world.

Where Can I Receive More Free Entrepreneur Information?

SUCCESS **DNA**

Sign up to receive SuccessDNA's FREE e-newsletter, which features informative articles and entrepreneur resources. Visit www.successdna.com for more details.

How Can I Protect My Personal and Business Assets?

For information on forming corporations, limited liability companies and limited partnerships to protect your personal and business holdings in all 50 states, as well as useful tips and strategies, visit Nevada Corporate Center's web site, located at www.goconv.com, or call toll-free 1-877-683-9342.

Special Offer – Mention this book and receive a 5% discount on the basic formation fee.

N·E·V·A·D·A
CORPORATE
C·E·N·T·E·R
INCORPORATED

SuccessDNA Publications

Order Here to Receive our Quality Business and Financial Books

ABCs for CEOs, written by Jet Parker, discusses the 26 key skills every business leader must possess.

The Cave Creed, written by Frank Troppe, discusses the importance of Competence, Agreement, Vigor and Execution in employment relationships.

Design/Build Your Business, written by Ron Sacchi, provides the blueprints for starting and succeeding in business.

Get Off the Couch!, written by Kenji Sax, Ph.D., shows how to use psychology for success in Business.

The Healthy Executive, written by Amy Sutton, is a complete explanation and method for attaining and maintaining your most important asset, your physical health. Topics from diet to exercise are presented in an easy-to-read and practical manner.

How to Use Limited Liability Companies & Limited Partnerships, written by Garrett Sutton, Esq. This publication is an in-depth study of how the special characteristics of limited liability partnerships may be used to your advantage for asset protection and wealth management.

The SuccessDNA Guide to Real Estate Investment and Management, written by Dolf de Roos, Ph.D. and Garrett Sutton, Esq., offers practical information on the essential elements of real estate acquisition and ownership.

Order Form

☐ **Please send me:**

____ *ABCs for CEOs* at $19.95 each
____ *The Cave Creed* at $19.95 each
____ *Design/Build Your Business* at $24.95 each
____ *Get Off the Couch!* at $17.95 each
____ *The Healthy Executive* at $19.95 each
____ *How to Use Limited Liability Companies & Limited Partnerships* at $19.95 each
____ *The SuccessDNA Guide to Real Estate Investment and Management* at $17.95 each

Please add $6.95 shipping and handling per book (NV residents please add 7.375% sales tax). Non-US orders must be accompanied by a money order in US funds. Allow 15 days for delivery.

My check or money order for $_____ is enclosed.

Please charge my ☐ VISA ☐ MasterCard ☐ American Express

Name: _____

Address: _____

City/State/Zip: _____

Phone: _____ Email: _____

Card # _____ Exp Date: _____

Signature: _____

Please make your check or money order payable and return to:
SuccessDNA Inc. ♦ PO Box 1450 ♦ Verdi, NV 89439
To order by credit card, call 1-800-293-7411 or fax to 1-775-824-0105
Also visit www.successdna.com to order books, tapes and other materials or to sign up for our e-newsletter!